FISH CAMP FAIL

**GO
FISHING** ▶ **CONTROL
THE FEAR** ▶ **AVOID
WEREWOLVES**

BEN JAILLER

For Pete

Contents

BEFORE

Of Mousers and Men

These men are hated. Despised. Ostracised. They're Cheats, no better than cormorants. They've been put under surveillance, grassed on, abused, attacked and banned. And do you know what? Not one fuck is given.

Meet Bristol Water's infamous Mousers. You won't find Eddie, Martin and the boys at Chew or Blagdon, mind. Their manor is the Barrow Tanks: three concrete bowl reservoirs bisected by the A38. Unforgiving waters fished by unforgiving blokes. Out there every day, in all weather, from dusk till dawn, caning in the fish and courting controversy.

A former topographer from Zimbabwe, Eddie has previous for being classed as an enemy. Having joined the opposition party against Robert Mugabe, he was forced to leave the country in 2002 and ended up settling in Bristol, where his daughter had married a local.

'A few years back, some of the nymph men got a petition against what they called the Mouse,' he says. 'They had T-shirts made with "Ban the Mouse" written on the front and stuck flyers on car windscreens. It was quite ridiculous.'

Following these protests, the future of the Mouse was debated and put to a vote in an extraordinary meeting held at Chew Valley Lodge.

'We lost out by seventy-seven votes to something,' Eddie continues. 'There aren't even seventy-seven blokes who fish the tanks! We said, "Look, if you're going to do it, do it fair and proper. Just ask the regulars who fish the tanks." The people who voted were the nymph men who fish Chew and Blagdon, not the regulars who fish the tanks. We were had on that one.'

So, what was all the fuss about? To find out, we have to go back to Young Ken, the man credited with inventing the Barrows Mouse more than fifty years ago. Legend has it that he couldn't for the life of him tie a muddler minnow and thus the Mouse was born.

'The original was made with pure white deer hair, with a red Antron or number four floss tail,' Eddie explains. 'Over the years, we started improving on it. When a mate found a whole stack of different-coloured deer hair in a shop in Wales, we started tying what we called the Hedgehog and put proper tails on.'

Hedgehog or Mouse, picture a Frankenstein's Monster of a reversed rodent, with a lone metal eye staring out of its arse and a tail emerging from what would be its nose. Eddie has always tied his own flies and for him it's the colour that seems to be the main attractor for the Mouse. In the past, he's used imitative colours, like golden olive with strands of krystal flash in the tail, and even tied a Mouse that represented the colours of a perch. While at the other end of the spectrum, there's one he calls the Kingfisher, with a blue head, white body and fluorescent orange tail.

'It was originally tied on a size six hook, but I now tie it on a ten or twelve because we found the smaller size more successful,' he says. 'One of my old favourites is what we call the bog standard. Yellow head, white body and a red tail. It still catches an awful lot of fish.'

An awful lot? Try shitloads of fish.

Therein lay the start of the controversy surrounding the Mouse. Eddie estimates that he's caught more than 1,000 in a season, both stockies and grown-on fish, but he's keen to stress that he wasn't breaking any rules. As a season ticket holder, he could take home eight sizeable fish every day and that's exactly what he did.

Martin may have been born in Malta, but he's 100% British Bulldog. Standing at not much over five-feet tall in his frayed Bootfoot neoprene waders, it's not the size of the dog in the fight, but the size of the fight in the dog and Young Marty, as he is affectionately known, is a fierce protector of Eddie and the other Mousers.

A coarse fisherman since the age of nine, it was his brother's father-in-law who got Martin into fly fishing on a trip to Hawkridge.

'I got to know Eddie and the other old-timers when I started fishing at the Barrows,' he says. 'There were eight of them, the youngest one being seventy-two, and they all fished the Mouse, which is what the nymph men started calling it.

'I was still young enough to fish nymphs and pull lures, but what converted me was the success rate. It was absolutely fantastic. They were catching a hell of a lot more fish than anyone else. People at the time were saying things, accusing them of putting stuff on the Mouse, which I didn't believe.

'A lot of people were jealous of the amount of fish being caught by them. The chap running the petition came up to me and asked would I like to sign. "No way – never," I said. The simple reason was that they were old, the poor buggers. Half the time, I'd carry their gear from the car park and up the bank to wherever they were fishing.

'You have to understand that the people who were

anti-Mouse were a hell of a lot younger than the ones who were fishing it. Unpleasant things were done and said. As I was younger, they never said anything to me, but yes, the other Mousers were picked on.'

The success of the Mouse was only half the controversy; the rest was how the mousers fished it. Eddie is left-handed, but unless you watched him for over an hour, you'd never know it. That's because his rod spends 99% of its time lying on the concrete lip of the reservoir, with a sinking line extending from the tip down into the water. The only time it's in his hand is when he's recasting or hauling in a trout.

Through trial and error, Young Ken discovered that the Mouse was most effective when fished static. Back in the day, Eddie used to take the head off a forty-plus line and attach it to an Amnesia shooting line, but now he favours a WF 8/9 rod with a Di-7 line. In winter, when the fish are down on the bottom, he will attach an 18" leader to the line with one Mouse on the point and another on the dropper. The length of the leader will increase as the water warms up and Eddie has even been known to use a 30ft leader to put his Mouse just under the surface, essentially fishing upside down.

'We found the hotspots by trial and error, or through watching other blokes fishing,' Eddie says. 'You just whack it out and leave it. The further you can get, the better – especially when the weed comes up. It's successful all-year round, and when the fish are on the move, you can bag up very quickly.'

After losing the vote, the Mousers were confined to tank number three. They could still fish the other two tanks with the Mouse, but number three was the only place where it could be fished static. As Eddie recalls: 'Four of us were banned for a week for not obeying the rules. The fishing was really poor on number three, so one day, we went and fished number one. We got fed up of retrieving the Mouse and all had our rods down. One of the nymph men complained to the fishery manager, who came out armed with a telescope. He saw us with our rods down, came charging over and that was it. We were banned.'

When tank number three was closed for maintenance, the Mousers were then banished to number one. After a second run-in with a ranger, who wasn't impressed by them taking ten minutes to bring their line back in on tank number two, the infamous three-minute rule was brought in for fishing on the other tanks. From casting and allowing the line to hit the bottom, the Mousers now had 180 seconds to retrieve their fly and recast.

'We had to have eyes in the back of our heads to keep a look out for the rangers and it was an opportunity for the nymph men to make things difficult for us,' Eddie says. 'There was one guy called the Poacher, who always fished the pipe on number three. If he saw us fishing it, he'd call the lodge, tell them we were fishing static and get us chased off so he could fish it.'

It's time I fessed up: I was one of the haters. If I saw a Mouser on the water, I would blank them. In my eyes, the way they plundered the water of fish made them no better than cormorants. Their way of fishing was as aesthetic as a shit on a swan's back; as close to the spirit of fly fishing as chucking a grenade into the water and scooping up the dead fish with a trawler net. I believed the stories about them putting baby oil on the Mouse to increase its buoyancy; about the empty jars of Marmite revealed on the bottom of the reservoir when the water levels dropped. Every time I saw a youngster being indoctrinated into the ways of the Mouse, I felt like Obi-Wan Kenobi watching Anakin Skywalker go over to the dark side.

Most serious of all, they didn't obey the rules of the fishery. If they were fishing where they shouldn't, I'd report them; likewise if they weren't retrieving their fly. I even resorted to filming them leaving their rods unattended. It started to affect my enjoyment of fishing at the Barrows. I found myself thinking more about catching Mousers breaking the rules than catching fish. It got to the point where I couldn't stand being on the same piece of water as them, all of which was a bit strange when, in every other area of life, my heroes have always been rebels: Kerouac, Bukowski, Brando, Klaus Kinski, Peckinpah, Herzog, Viv Richards, Botham, Best and Cantona – sticking two fingers up to convention and authority. Yet here I was hating on a bunch of old men for doing exactly that. These Mousers were true rebels in every sense of the word.

Who are you to tell us how we should fish? Who are you to tell us where we can fish? We'll fish however and wherever we fucking want, Jack! It's a paying fishery. We pay our money to catch fish. What's the fucking difference whether you use nymphs, the Mouse or whatever?

They are to JR Hartley what the Sex Pistols were to Ed Grundy, telling the tweed-jacketed twat to go stick his nymphs up his arse. I should've been applauding them, not hating them. How did I get it so wrong that putting on my fly vest transformed me from Keith Richards into Cliff Richard?

Fast forward to the new season. It's the week before the World Cup in Russia, and I'm sandwiched between Eddie and Martin on Boy's Corner. My rod is lying on the floor with a Mouse on the end of my Di-5, and we're chatting shit about everything from the hidden benefits of a blue badge to Maltese planning regulations and the top-five most poisonous snakes on the planet. Even though it's early June, Eddie is sporting more layers than the Jurassic Coast. With his fleece hat pulled down to the brim of his glasses, and his white beard as overgrown as a hoarder's garden, the only pieces of flesh that are exposed to the elements are his nose and cheeks. He's been out here every day for the last sixteen years, and the lines and broken blood vessels on his face now resemble the contours, rivers and tributaries he used to mark on his maps back in his beloved 'Zim.'

So, what led to this change of heart? Well, two things. Both were viral videos that I watched back-to-back on *YouTube*. The first was of a young lady on a New Jersey beach being questioned by a cop about underage drinking. Things escalate quickly after she refuses to give her name and the video ends with the cop repeatedly punching her in the head, getting her in a chokehold and pinning her down in the sand while a colleague cuffs her. The second video is from the helmet cam of a motorcyclist in central London. The biker is heading down the road between two lines of queuing traffic, and as he moves alongside a double-decker bus, the driver suddenly puts his hand out of the window to warn him that a pedestrian is about to step out from in front of the bus. The biker brakes, lets the pedestrian cross in front of him, exchanges a fist bump with the bus driver and continues his journey.

Now, the video of the young lady and the cop on the beach featured numerous instances where the story could have had a very different ending, but they were both clearly having a bad day and neither was prepared to back down. The young lady was affronted by having her day at the beach interrupted and the cop wasn't going to have his authority challenged. The ending was as inevitable as a Jose Mourinho third season meltdown. Similarly, the helmet cam video could also have ended differently. The bus driver might have failed to warn the biker out of contempt for the everyday stupidity of people, leading to the biker abusing the pedestrian for stepping out in front of him or the pedestrian confronting the biker for driving dangerously. Before they know it, they're fodder for a Channel 5 show with the word 'Angriest' in the title.

The lessons I took from this experience were that you should always give your name to New Jersey cops, and make sure to stop and look when stepping out from in front of a stationary London bus. Oh, and also that a lack of appreciation of someone else's perspective will inevitably lead to conflict. The two protagonists in the beach video behaved despicably, but they aren't necessarily bad people. I'm sure that they are both loved and capable of loving, and I'm pretty sure that neither of them has ever strangled a kitten.

As it turns out, neither have Eddie or Martin. Eddie has been a widower since 2004. He used to enjoy days out with his wife and the grandkids to Ashton Court, particularly when the balloon and kite festivals were on. He smiles at the memory. 'It's fair to say that fishing has taken over my life since my wife died. I don't mean I'm a fanatical fisherman, but it's more an excuse to get out of the flat. I hate to sit there staring at the four walls all day – I'd much rather be out here. Rain, shine or hail, you name it, we're out here fishing. If we catch a fish, we catch a fish. If we don't, we're still happy.'

Unbeaten, unapologetic and unbowed, the Mousers once again have the freedom to fish static on all three tanks. It's a hollow victory, though, as there aren't many of them left now.

Eddie England, John Taylor, Hospital Ken and Young Ken have all gone. Martin, who is considered a youngster, is in his mid-sixties and Eddie's health has taken a turn for the worse in recent months. An eighty-a-day cigarette man in his youth, he struggles to make it up the steps to tank number three these days, but thankfully, just like he was for the other Mousers when their bodies began to fail them, Martin is now there for Eddie, carrying his gear up from the car and supporting him when he pauses to catch his breath. Martin lost his own father at a very young age. He's been married for forty years, tends his allotment on Mondays and Tuesdays, and spends time with his wife on Thursdays and Fridays. His fishing days are Wednesday, Saturday and Sunday without fail.

'My friendship with Eddie means a hell of a lot to me,' Martin says. 'He's like the father I never had, and I always look forward to seeing him and all the others at the tanks. The enjoyment we get out of it is unbelievable. I've fished all my life and I love it.'

Like the dwindling band of Mousers, the Barrows also feels as though it's coming to an end. The problems at Bristol Water have been well documented and the future of the Barrows is uncertain, with even the idea of it housing floating solar panels having been proposed by the men in suits. One thing is certain, however: the heady days of Eddie catching a thousand fish in a season are long gone. On the day I join him and Martin, they haven't caught a fish all week.

'Every season, there's been less and less fish being stocked,' he says. 'Going back a few years, there'd be between two and three hundred cormorants on number three. Now, you don't see a single one. To us, no cormorants means no fish.'

It's been a few years since Bristol Water has had what the Mousers refer to as a 'proper' fisheries manager. The air of neglect around the Barrows is palpable, from the derelict returns hut to the complete lack of disabled access, and there's even sympathy from the Mousers for the nymph men, who are unable to fish during the summer months due to weed growth.

'Our main concern is that the fishery doesn't pack in,' Eddie says. 'If they can attract more youngsters to fish then it will continue. We encourage the youngsters here to fish not just the Mouse, but all methods. My grandson loved fishing the Mouse, but eventually said, "Granddad, can I put the floater on?" I said, "No problem," and he caught his first fish off the ramp on a little damsel nymph that I tied.'

The question is, will the Mouse and the fishery that gave birth to it both survive? Or, more to the point, *should* they survive? As fly fishing rightly moves towards conserving fish stocks rather than catch-and-kill, perhaps the Mouse shouldn't outlive the individuals that have fished it to such deadly effect.

Similar to how Eddie finds himself suffering painfully for all those Capstan Full Strength smoked in his youth, the current famine at the Barrows is a result of years of excessive feasting, where more fish were taken per season than any one person could ever eat. Just because you could doesn't mean you should, and that applies as much to the sins of our youth as it does to our plunder of the planet's natural resources. Eddie and the Barrows stand as testimony to the fact that the heady days of buy now, pay later have gone. The bill has come in and the price now has to be paid.

I hope that with Marty at his side to help him up the stairs, Eddie will continue to keep those four walls from closing in on him for as long as he possibly can – and I know that every day he sits with his rod at his feet, chatting shit with the other Mousers and waiting for that tug on the end of his line, will taste like champagne.

Ginny vs the Four French Bulldogs of the Apocalypse

I didn't know that ferry staff collected empty coffee cups. Or were polite. Or even smiled. Years of travelling on Brittany Ferries, crewed by surly French teens, have seriously lowered my expectations of maritime customer service, but the *Finlaggan* is different. It also has a priority seating area for dogs and their owners. I hadn't realised this when I sat down. All I saw was the most amazing amount of leg room I've ever seen in my entire life.

I know that I shouldn't be sitting here. It's not just that I don't own a dog. It's also because of how I feel about dogs. A cartoon by Brian Bolland titled *Shit the Dog* sums it up perfectly. In panel one, the afore mentioned Shit is licking his balls. In panel two, he's moved on to his bum. Panel three shows him licking a man's hand and the final panel shows the same man selling an excited teenager a hamburger from his burger van.

The men's tennis semi of the Queen's Club Championship is on the TV. Both players are receiving treatment between games. It's less about who's going to win and more about which one is going to quit first. I didn't get much sleep in the B&B in Moffat last night. It sounded like the person in the room above mine was coughing up a lung. I've necked an espresso, hoping the caffeine will keep me awake, but all it does is set my already frayed nerves even more on edge. The alarm on a camper van blares every thirty seconds on repeat.

I'm twitchier than Steve Smith at the crease and my need to disconnect from the wider world is more urgent than ever.

One of a pair of Border terriers climbs down off the seat in front of me and begins attacking the laces of my Vans. A neurotic spaniel belonging to a young couple whines and shakes when the girl goes to the restaurant at the bow of the ship. A Cheshire housewife parades up and down the deck with four French bulldogs wearing what looks like matching black leather S&M gear. A white hound the size of Tyson Fury sleeps on the deck with one eye open, waiting for one of the bulldogs to come within its range. The air is filled with yips, barks, growls and whimpers. There are too many dogs in too small a space and there's that feeling of impending violence you get in a kebab shop at 2am on a Friday night.

I'll soon be on a remote Scottish island with fewer people on it than there are dog owners on this ferry and I cannot fucking wait.

There's a mini JCB trundling up the same track I've just abandoned my Mazda 3 on after grounding the chassis on a rock. It shouldn't have surprised me that driving to Home Loch on the Ardlussa Estate wasn't like driving up to the lodge at Chew Valley. It looked straightforward enough on the map: turn right out of Otter Cottage onto the main road, drive around the bend, over Lussa River and then left onto a track that runs in a straight line to the loch; but if my time on Jura has taught me anything, it's that nothing's easy here. There are no straight lines. No shortcuts. You won't survive looking for the easiest way to do things because the easy way doesn't exist here. Everything takes effort. Tussocks that can break an ankle. Bogs where you can disappear up to your hip without warning. And I haven't seen a loaf of bread during my entire stay on the island.

Home Loch is teardrop-shaped, with a dam at the end nearest the track. At either end of the dam are a pair of rusty bridges sitting on ancient stone bases. They cross a pair of streams flowing out of the loch to allow the Lussa River to continue its course to the sea. In the far corner, there's a weather-beaten boat shed with a rusty, corrugated-iron roof that has seen better days, and a green rowboat moored up next to a lily bed. The westerly bank sits at the base of a hill and is a twisted maze of rhododendrons. The opposite bank is flat moorland and at the far end of the loch stands Cruach Lonnastail, which peaks at 1,000ft. Above all this is a blazing sun in a cloudless blue sky, turning the peaty-coloured water into its mirror image.

With 90% of my fish caught during this holiday on a Black Pennell and the rest either taking a Bibio or Kate McLaren, I see no point in changing things now, so I go with my usual 5Wt set up with a floating line. I cross the stone bridge and tackle up on the dam wall. The Pennell goes on the first dropper and I put a Kate McLaren on the point. What wind there is blows off the moorland bank from left to right and there are fish rising in a bay to my right. I'm never comfortable fishing solo in a boat and with no life jacket, it's not like I need a rising fish to convince me that bank is best.

I wade across the stream's shallow bed and work my way down the moorland bank, casting and moving, and soon realise that I can't go any further without walking around a large bay where the guy in the JCB is digging a rectangular hole in the boggy ground. He switches off the digger's engine as I approach. He's tall and slim, with grey hair poking out from beneath a denim, short-peaked engineer's cap, bringing to mind an image of James Coburn at his most laconic, to whom he bears more than a passing resemblance. His name's Ewen. He's the head stalker on the Ardlussa Estate and he's digging the foundations for a new boathouse to replace the ramshackle one at the far end of the dam. I ask him if it's better to fish from the bank or the boat.

'The tussocks are hard going, so it's best to take the boat. You can always moor it up and fish from the bank further down the loch if you want.'

Luckily, the rowboat is in better condition than the old boathouse. It's also light and made of plastic, so even someone like me should be able to handle it. I still have flashbacks to the first time I took one of the heavy wooden rowboats out at Blagdon and rowed down towards the dam end before realising I didn't have the strength to row it back against a stiff north-easterly wind. I had to beach it and phone for an engine to be delivered from the local pub, like I was ordering from Mission Burrito on Deliveroo.

I'm casting tight up against the rhododendrons overhanging the far bank when I become aware of eyes on my back. Not just on my back – the feeling is more like a pair of laser beams burning through my shoulder blades and roasting my lungs. I let the boat drift around and see a black-and-white sprocker spaniel sitting on a rocky outcrop at the dam end of the loch. I think the correct term for how gun dogs sit when alert is 'erect.' Well, this one takes it to a whole new level. It's like someone mixed Viagra into its Pedigree Chum this morning.

I look around to see if there's one of the red deer that feed on the grass outside Otter Cottage every evening knocking around, but there's nothing. It's me who's the sole focus of her attention. She's so unnaturally still that I'm half expecting her fur to start rippling, her face to peel open like a banana and a

Rob Bottin special effects masterpiece to erupt from inside.

I wonder if, like in an episode of *Skippy the Bush Kangaroo*, there's been a disaster at an abandoned mine, and she wants me to follow her to save whoever is trapped below ground. My next thought is that something has happened to Ewen in the mini JCB, but he's still happily digging away, so what does this mutt want?

I row towards her, and when I'm within fifty feet of the shore, she jumps into the water and swims towards the boat. She's the size of a large sheep and there's no way I'm getting her in without capsizing. I don't know how long dogs can swim and I'm worried that if she gets too tired to swim back to the shore, she might drown. I've no choice now but to row back to the shore and hope that she follows. Luckily, she does just that, swimming happily alongside me until I beach the boat in the shallows. Then, she jumps aboard, shakes herself dry and sits down in the stern.

A Mexican standoff develops between me and the dog, who has gone back into Husky from *The Thing* mode. I get out of the boat and try to encourage her to do likewise, patting my thighs and saying, 'C'mon.'

Nothing. I offer her a piece of leftover Argyll Slice. Not interested.

'What?'

The dog sits there, unmoving, staring straight ahead.

'Want to go fishing?'

She doesn't move a hair, but there's the merest flicker in her eyes as they dart to starboard and momentarily meet mine. I push the boat back out into the loch and jump in.

'Guess we're going fishing, then.'

I row the length of the dam and the dog never takes her eyes off the water. I'm positive she's looking for fish, but then

I notice she's staring at something. I turn around in the boat to follow her gaze and see the lily beds in the far corner of the loch opposite a derelict boat shed.

'What's that, Skip? There's fish in the lilies?'

I set up a drift along the lily beds. Casting along its outer edge, I quickly pick up two fish; one to the Kate McLaren on point and one to my go-to fly for the holiday, a Black Pennell. Each brownie gets a kiss from me and a lick from her before I slip them back into the water. Despite the midday sun, one or two fish begin to rise. The dog hears the rise almost before the fish breaks the surface. There's no need to call out angles on the clock face. I just cast in whatever direction she's looking.

The dog seems like she could stay out here all day, but with the takes drying up, I want to put something heavier on the point and fish the deeper water from the dam wall. We both jump out of the boat and the dog shadows me as I work my back up along the dam wall. We're both so engrossed in the fishing that it's only when Ewen appears on the far bridge and whistles for her that I notice the absence of engine noise. The dog does a remarkable impersonation of my daughter playing *Roblox* on her Kindle and completely ignores Ewen, forcing him to walk the length of the dam to reach us. Still the dog ignores his calls. At one point, she actually hides behind me like a kid who doesn't want to stop playing football and go home for their tea.

It turns out that the dog is Ewen's. Her name is Ginny. I tell him it's my last day tomorrow and ask if there's anywhere he could recommend I fish. He tells me that many years ago, he stocked some brown trout in a remote hill loch and promptly forgot about them. Then, a few years later, he walked past the loch and saw some very big fish in there. He's going there tomorrow with Ginny and invites me along.

Streamers, my 7wt and big-boy net are compulsory.

For me, coming to Jura was as much a form of exorcism as it was an act of escapism, but there is an ancient, reptilian part of my brain that I'm not sure Father Karras could cleanse, let alone an island with a population of two hundred people.

I was fine with the thought of holidaying solo right up until I realised there were no keys in my holiday cottage to lock either the front or back doors. I've spent years living in cities where a healthy level of paranoia is essential to your everyday survival. Trouble is, my paranoia, fuelled by years of watching horror films, made it impossible for me to sleep soundly knowing the doors downstairs were unlocked. So, from my first night on Jura, I've slept with a wooden chair wedged under the handle of the porch door. I also leant my rod tubes against the PVC-framed back door. It opens inwards, so my reasoning is that an intruder can't enter Otter Cottage without sending my rods clattering to the tiled floor and waking me up. What I would do upon being alerted, I never figure out, but I slept with my Gransfors Hatchet under my pillow just in case.

With my car abandoned at literally Road End, and the Argo Cat I've been sitting in for the last fifty minutes climbing steadily over the moorland, that same part of my psyche casually pops the phrase "Keep off the moors. Stick to the roads" into my mind. It may be a blazing sun overhead instead of a full moon, but suddenly I'm hearing a familiar howl in my head, and I'm pretty sure there's no coyotes on Jura.

What if they were all in on it? I begin to think.

The wonderful people of Jura could not have been more welcoming and if that welcome was intended to lull me into a false sense of security, it worked. Truth is, I've fallen for this island as hard as a Jura brownie for a Black Pennell. The postcard to my partner and daughter, informing them that I am never coming back, was written on the first evening; my method of disappearance to be less Reggie Perrin and more Colonel Kurtz. Any potential Captain Willard's dispatched to terminate my command would find me shaven-headed, wearing black PJs and reciting William Blake to red deer, my methods for catching wild brown trout having become unsound.

However, I'm beginning to fear my disappearance is about to become more permanent. I'm 560 miles, two ferries and one overnight stop from home. There's no mobile phone signal. I'm in the remotest part of a remote island with someone I've known for all of five minutes. There are no witnesses. That howling in my head is joined by the sound of Duelling Banjos and a vision of a wicker man appearing over the next rise.
What better way to lure an unsuspecting fly fisherman to his death than with the promise of a secret loch and huge trout?

Given my tendency towards horror-fuelled paranoia, you won't be surprised that, under ordinary circumstances, I would never put myself in such a vulnerable position. Saying that, it was no less unlikely – given my meltdown in the canine priority seating area – that only twenty-four hours earlier, I was happily sharing a boat with a four-legged botulism factory.

Only fly fishing can do this to me. Add fly fishing to any situation, and I'm instantly disarmed of my worst prejudices and most paranoid fears. This is because anyone or anything that fly fishes can't be all bad. If Fred West had had a Bristol Water Fisheries sticker in the back window of his van, I'd have happily accepted a lift from him. If President Bolsonaro fished for Peacock Bass in the Amazon instead of setting fire to it, I'd happily put a big fat 'X' next to the ego-maniacal, Brazilian bell-end's name. Likewise, if the Emperor swapped his red lightsaber for a Sage X at weekends and fished the seas of Kamino, I'd happily don a white stormtrooper's helmet and fight for the evil Empire.

Like me, Ewen is a fly fisherman and a shared love of fly fishing is like the ultimate Masonic handshake. Fly fisherman don't murder people. A fly fisherman wouldn't destroy an ecosystem or build a death star; obliterate entire planets or enslave a galaxy far, far away. In short, fly fishermen aren't dicks, so deep down, I know there's no wicker man and that Ewen won't be complimenting me on my moobies. Instead, there will be a secret lake stuffed with huge, wild brown trout.

Ewen's loch is a glacial scar, shaped like a human heart. It's barely an acre in size, but the cliff face that runs the length of the western bank tells me that it's deep enough to support fish the size that Ewen has spoken of. I don't know who's more excited, me or Ginny, as I string up my 7wt with a clear, slow-sinking intermediate, tie on a Grizzle Snake and strap my big boy net to my sling pack.

This is the highest up I've been on Jura. I can see two of the lochs I've fished previously hundreds of feet below us and beyond them the Isle of Scarba. The air is so clear, I can make out a lone house on the tiny island. Ewen tells me that if he ever wins the lottery, he's going to buy it.

'So no fucker can annoy me,' he says.

He may be a fellow fly fisherman, but I make a mental note not to piss him off.

Ewen's father was the head stalker on the Ardlussa Estate before him, and apart from a six-year stint in the merchant navy, he's lived his entire life on Jura. I ask him what he misses most about the mainland.

'Decent bread and a haircut,' he answers.

He used to get fresh bread every day in the merchant navy and his wife gets so fed up with his hair that she ends up cutting it herself. Oh, and if you ever meet him driving his

Land Rover on the single-track road that runs the length of the island, I suggest you reverse your vehicle as quickly as possible into the nearest passing bay.

Apparently, Ginny always follows the fisherman who catches the most fish, so of course, she sticks to Ewen, right up until the moment I take the first fish of the day – a brownie barely bigger than the Grizzle Snake – the shameless hussy.

I'm letting the fly sink deep and getting the occasional nip, but that's all. The wind is gusting diagonally across the loch from the south-east, which isn't a problem for a right-hander, but things get trickier as I fish my way around the aorta and into a second, smaller bay, which has me casting into the face of the gale. Ginny is long gone. She displayed a loyalty far beyond my ability as a fly fisherman. I'm relieved that she's not here to see how inept my casting is. I can barely get a line out. Then, something straight out of *Jurassic Park* whacks my fly and is gone before I can strike. I couldn't tell you if it was a tyrannosaurus, triceratops or velociraptor, but minutes later, my hands are still vibrating like that glass of water on the dashboard of Tim and Lex's Ford Explorer.

The combination of the gusting wind and cloudless blue sky gives me the feeling that it's not going to be our day. By 6pm, even Ewen's legendary desire for solitude is flagging. Ginny, as ever, puts us to shame with her dedication. She sits motionless, ignoring Ewen's calls to come and stares into the depths of the lake where the only monsters on the island lurk.

I know that getting into the Argo Cat will mark the start of my journey back into the madness. The strong south-easterly wind blows across the moor, directly into my face. I can taste the pollen on my tongue. My eyes are streaming and I try to tell myself it's because I ran out of hay fever spray two days ago.

Like Ginny, I don't want to go. Perhaps the vision of being butchered, buggered or burnt to death in a wicker man was part of my subconscious desire to stay on the island. In twelve hours' time, when I'm back on the *Finlaggan* with the unsent postcard to my family in my pocket, and four French bulldogs in matching S&M gear humping my leg, I'll conclude that if being buggered, butchered or burnt to death is what it would've taken for me to stay, that would have been fine with me.

As long as I'm reincarnated as a fishing-mad sprocker called Ginny.

Looking for fun and action ?
(read on back for more)

Bay of the Dead

The hardest video game I've ever played is *Dark Souls*. If there's a Hollywood reboot of the legend of Sisyphus, he won't be pushing a boulder up a hill for all eternity. He'll be stuck in Anor Londo without any poison arrows, trying to get past the two archers.

At the start of the game, you're dumped in a world of the undead. You're kitten-weak, with nothing but a broken sword and a wooden shield to defend yourself. There's no manual and no help screen. You have no idea what you're supposed to do or where you're supposed to go and everything wants to kill you.

When you die, the words 'You died' appear on the screen. I saw those two words so often, they were the last thing I saw at night when I closed my eyes and the first thing I saw before I opened them in the morning, which particularly freaked me out. And there are so many frustratingly ridiculous ways to die.

There's an early level in the game called the Undead Burg, which involves fighting your way through a decaying medieval town. After taking on Hollows, Hollow Warriors throwing firebombs, Undead Soldiers (both swords and spears) and fighting a Black Knight (like trying to cast at, play and land a Tarpon on a 3WT in a hurricane), I came to a steep set of stairs leading up to a tower, down which, without warning, rolled a flaming barrel that immediately killed me.

In *Dark Souls*, every death is a school day, so I now knew that the next time I went up those stairs, a flaming barrel would roll down, and after fighting my way through Hollows, Hollow Warriors throwing firebombs, Undead Soldiers (both sword and spears) and staying as far away as I can from the Black Knight (having realised the futility of taking on a Tarpon with a 3WT in a hurricane), I again came to the steep set of stairs leading up to the tower.

Everything in *Dark Souls* is there for a reason and I'd noticed a gap in the wall that runs alongside the steps. I reasoned that I am supposed to jump through that gap in the wall when the flaming barrel (with warning this time) rolls down the steps. I timed my leap to perfection and dodged the flaming barrel, except I missed the ledge below, which I was supposed to safely land on.

'You died.'

The only way to progress through the game is to gain souls, which you do by killing your enemies. By resting at bonfires located throughout the game, you spend your accumulated souls on XP (experience points). XP can be used to make your character stronger, faster, more agile or more intelligent; Gaining experience is how you take on and kill increasingly difficult enemies and progress through the game. Trouble is, the bonfires are few and far between. Some are so well hidden that you can walk straight past them without even knowing they are there. And here's the rub: if you get killed, all your accumulated souls are reduced to a bloodstain on the spot that you died. When you die, you respawn at the last bonfire you rested at and all the enemies you have killed also respawn along with you. If you then die before you can make it back to the bloodstain and reclaim your souls, you lose them all. And you will die, again and again and again.

Baie des Trépassés, on the western tip of Brittany, translates as 'Bay of the Dead.' Not only does it sound like a *Dark Souls* level, it also looks like it could've been designed by Hidetaka Miyazaki himself.

It's approaching 6am and the rising sun is obscured by dark clouds. I'm standing at the top of a cliff; the grass slope falls away vertically beneath my boots. In front, there's nothing between me and Newfoundland except a boiling, writhing ocean the colour of ash. If I could look down beyond the crumbling cliff edge, I'd see jagged seams of granite thrusting up vertically in the predawn light, like claws exploding from a grave, and I wish to Christ that I was playing a video game right now.

The trouble with real life is that you only get one chance. There's no respawning. I slip now and it really is game over.

My French fishing guide, Manu, is ten feet in front of me. He's actually leaning out into the void. His focus is on the rock platform two hundred feet down, where a lanky teenage kid is already fishing.

'Fucking hell,' he exclaims, 'I don't believe it. That guy is there every fucking day!'

If I was capable of being aware of anything else at this moment, it would be Manu's urge to climb down the cliff and gain some souls by throttling the life from this kid, but right now, I'm too preoccupied with a couple of urges of my own. One is the entirely irrational compulsion to throw myself over the edge of the cliff and the other is to throw up.

Did I mention that I get vertigo? It only started to affect me in my thirties, so I'm unsure if it's an inner-ear thing or just down to age. What I do know is if you put me in front of a steep drop, with nothing in front of me but a wide-open space, I will fall apart quicker than an Arsenal Premier League title challenge.

I should have had an inkling about what was in store

after a weekend visit to *La Pointe Du Raz*. It's France's answer to Land's End, but with a complete lack of any of the health and safety we're world famous for. Tourists swarmed all over the jagged dragon's spine of granite that juts out into the Atlantic, like suicidal lemmings. The mere sight of a family standing on the edge of a sheer drop taking selfies, or an unaccompanied toddler running about, made me want to chew my lips off.

My survival technique for coping with *La Pointe Du Raz* was the same as the one I used when coming across a Black Knight in *Dark Souls*. However, as Manu begins to head down to the rock platform, not going within fifty feet of a cliff edge isn't going to be an option today.

I can't even see any path that he's following. The grass slope is too steep and too dry to offer any purchase, so I'm reduced to sliding down on my arse, my fingers clutching at the crumbling sods of earth. It's all too much for me and I freeze as Manu reaches the start of the band of black rock. It takes all my effort just to stay where I am.

'Manu.'

'Are you OK?'

'I can't do it. Too steep.'

'You sure? It's real good fishing down there.'

'I can't.'

Even in the half-light, I can still make out the imperceptible Gallic shrug and then he's heading back up above me. I crawl after him on my hands and knees, until whoever replaced the bones in my legs with Rowntree's Strawberry Jelly takes pity on me and swaps them back.

It's hard to imagine now, but back when I lived in London, my summer holidays were the only time I fished. For my first holiday away with my partner in Oban, it was my coarse fishing gear that went in the boot, but after casting a fly on a small loch owned by a friend of the lady whose cottage we were renting, it was my fly gear that accompanied us on all subsequent holidays.

When we moved to Bristol and I started fishing regularly at the Barrows, it was decided that because I could now fish whenever I wanted, all holidays were to be fishing-free zones. Well, almost fish-free. The gentleman's agreement was that my fly gear could still go, but I was restricted to a single session at a local fishery, either in the evening or early morning.

The exception to this was Brittany, where my friend Julie had a static caravan at a Yelloh Village. With our daughter reaching school age and my finances facing the bend-over-and-grab-your-ankles economics of holidaying in the month of August, the offer of mates' rates made this an attractive proposition.

Yards from a crescent-shaped beach, with an indoor and outdoor pool, it was a case of 'water, water everywhere, but not a trout in sight,' so my rods stayed at home. However, over the next couple of years, my early morning drive down the coastal road to get bread and croissants became a cycle ride along the coastal path, bringing me into contact with the various harbours that dotted the coastline.

Gear or no gear, I was still a fisherman and unable to pass any body of water without giving it a scan through a pair of Polaroids. As I explored the harbours, I noticed the large numbers of fish that were gathered with the incoming tide. Beyond the mullet, I hadn't a clue what they were, but I resolved to bring some tackle with me the next time we came to Brittany.

As it happened, our next stay wasn't at the caravan. When I finally get around to writing my autobiography, it will probably be called *The Great Procrastinator*, so we not only missed out on booking Julie's caravan, but also a four-berth cabin on the night ferry and were limited to leftovers when it came to choosing an alternative destination. The best of the half-eaten sausage rolls within our price range was a single-storey fisherman's cottage in the medieval town of Pont-Croix.

Not only did Pont-Croix bear a spooky resemblance to the Undead Burg, it was also on the tidal estuary of the Goyen River, which a bit of research revealed is famed for its salmon, brown trout and sea trout. The tidal estuary and miles and miles of rocky coastline all screamed sea bass, plus there was the harbour of Audierne only a five-minute drive away, where I knew there would be mullet. All of this almost made up for the fact that on the night ferry over, I would be sleeping on the metal floor of the cabin.

It's my fifteenth year as a fly fisherman, and, as is customary with any milestone I reach, I've been busy unpicking my past and questioning my future direction. With the exception of fishing some small brooks south of Bath one season while I was working freelance, 98% of my fly fishing had been done on stocked reservoirs. Give or take a few pounds, the trout I was catching had become indistinguishable. Born in sterile hatcheries and grown on in cages, in my eyes these Frankenstein's Monsters were as unnatural and sexless as Donald Trump's marriage, so the idea of targeting something truly wild was very appealing.

I decided that catching a sea bass was the shot in the arm I needed to get over my fish-life crisis. Unfortunately, even the most cursory research revealed that the 'Ferrari and a sexual partner half my age' option of casting a fly for a day from a motorised skiff would cost almost as much as the price of renting our holiday cottage for a week.

Enter the new Manu in my life. Based just up the road

from Pont-Croix, not only did he have the same Christian name as one of my favourite-ever French players, he also matched my more realistic budget of a Citroen 2CV and 4am pick-up. We exchanged emails and I agreed to call him when I arrived in Pont-Croix to arrange a date.

But I didn't call him when I arrived. Not immediately anyway. The pound had plummeted. A litre of unleaded fuel was €1.51 at Super U. Three pizzas and drinks in the town square set me back £45. I was also holding out for a Lobster Thermidor or *Fruits de Mere* later in the holiday, so could I really justify spunking ninety quid on four hours' fishing? It's not just that; the difference in price was down to Manu favouring the spinner over the fly. If casting a dry fly to a rising trout was Monet painting *Woman With a Parasol*, chucking a lump of metal into the sea felt like the equivalent of spray painting a cock and balls on the side of a bus stop.

Instead, I strung up my 7WT with a clear intermediate and a softy sand eel and headed down to the town section of the estuary at low tide. Two hundred feet across at its widest point, the Goyen estuary had dropped twenty feet from its high-tide mark and was reduced to a coffee-coloured trickle between exposed mudbanks. There were fish at the edges, darting among the seaweed, but they were mullet rather than sea bass. I gave it a couple of hours before going back to the cottage. I told myself that it felt good just to be casting again.

Two early morning sessions saw me fishing the length of the Goyen Estuary from Pont-Croix to *L'Aquashow* outside Audierne. I couldn't even see a sea bass, let alone catch one, and I wasn't even sure if I'd recognise one if I did. Desperate to catch something, I resorted to casting at the mullet that swam beneath the stone bridge in Pont-Croix, which separated the freshwater section from the saltwater estuary. I hadn't prepared for fishing for mullet, though, and any flies that I might've had success with, such as red tags or an apps bloodworm, were back in my fly boxes at home. The only thing that might have worked was a river shrimp pattern that could, at a push, have resembled a prawn, and when I lost that on a frayed blue anchor rope attached to a wooden rowboat, I packed up and returned to the cottage. I told myself it felt good just to be casting again. It was a lie.

The next day, we were in Audierne to enquire about hiring a canoe. In England, a member of staff might politely ask a customer if they wouldn't mind awfully if they vacated the premises, as they need to close for lunch. In that deliciously arrogant French way, the staff in the tourist information centre just turned off the lights and disappeared. Left alone in the gloom, I spotted some neon-orange writing on a grey flyer, with a familiar face on the inside holding an enormous sea bass. It was Manu. The English copy on the back page read: 'Looking for action?' I slipped the flyer into my pocket as we shuffled out into the daylight.

I had less than a week of the holiday left to catch a sea bass. My clueless attempts at catching one had me feeling like I was eight years old again, fishing for minnows in a Welsh stream with a piece of tinfoil folded over a hook. It's a scary thing, facing the unknown with nothing but a broken sword and a wooden shield, but this time, I didn't have to do it alone. Fuck the Lobster Thermidor. It was time to Manu up.

A couple of days later, I met Manu in a deserted hotel car park that overlooked the beach at the Baie des Trépassés. The inside of his battered Citroen Xsara was as reassuringly shitty as only a true fishing guide's vehicle can be. It may have been missing the kind of detritus you'd usually only find washed-up ashore after a Tsunami, but there was an inch-thick layer of grime covering every surface and the gear nob was missing, having presumably been ripped off in a fit of rage and hurled at the driver of one of the locust-like motorhomes who, to his eternal disgust, clog up the narrow Brittany roads, parked in passing bays and contributed nothing to the local economy. Worse still, as he reminded me later, he'd been guiding for eleven years and only ever had two clients from among their legion.

Manu had been a professional musician, playing double bass in the jazz clubs of Paris before returning to his childhood home in Brittany to take up guiding. He told me that he learnt English from American jazz musicians, 'So everything is "fucking A," "fucking B" and "fucking C."'

After years of having hairy-arsed Frenchman driving an inch from my bumper, I finally got to experience riding in a car with one of them. I couldn't have been more terrified if I was a passenger in a Lancia Delta S4 being driven by Stevie Wonder in the Portuguese Rally, while Helen Keller navigated. I was pinned to my seat by what felt like 9Gs. I knew we had to take the next turn on the left, but Manu gave no indication to reassure me that he was safely going to make it, such as braking or indicating. He waited until my fingertips were embedded in the dashboard, Steve Martin-style, and we were parallel with the turn before he power-slid across the junction, all the while articulating an unbroken stream of consciousness regarding the effect that the collapsing Gulf Stream was having on the ocean, and the impact of the recent influx of people fleeing the killer heatwave that had fried the rest of France.

Apparently, it had been an unusually cold summer in Brittany, with no prolonged spells of settled weather, which had had an adverse effect on the fishing, so he was literally taking things day-by-day. My trip had to be postponed until near the end of the holiday after yet another storm battered the west coast, meaning that we had to wait for the sea to clear of debris. He wanted the tourists to come for his guiding business to thrive, but not at the expense of balance. The lanes were too narrow, the car parks too small and there wasn't the infrastructure to cope with the number of people seeking relief from temperatures inland that topped 42° in July. Too many visitors would run the risk of destroying the remoteness and tranquillity that Brittany is famous for.

Manu didn't want it turning into Disney World.

It's only on the walk of shame away from the cliff that I get my first good look at Manu's face. Up until then, it has been shrouded in the hood of his fishing jacket, leaving me with the feeling that I would either be fishing with him from the rocks or, if I fell, playing chess with him on the shore.

Whether it's nature or nurture, Manu is perfectly adapted to his environment. His resemblance to a mountain goat extends beyond his mastery of the cliffs; he has a gaunt, narrow face, with drawn-back lips unable to cover an impressive set of teeth. Combined with his slight build and stick-thin legs, if his cap ever came off, I wouldn't be a surprise to see a pair of hoary horns poking up through his browny-blond hair.

We're fishing an area north of the Baie des Trépassés, where two opposing points of the coast form the snarling jaws of a wolverine, with a narrow bay as the mouth. It was descending the underside of the lower jaw which reduced me to a puddle and as Manu stops at the top of the cliff, I'm still unsure if he's going to call it a day in disgust. Instead, he turns left before we reach the car and starts heading down to what would be the inside of the bottom jaw.

right hand in order to release the line. I try invoking the muscle memory of my coarse fishing days and hold the braid first under just my forefinger, and then both my forefinger and middle finger prior to releasing the line. On my first few attempts, the lure keeps crashing onto the rocks in front of my feet. I can't for the life of me work out why I can't do this. Perhaps it's because I've never done anything fishing-related with my right hand except grip a fly rod. For my previously dormant digits, it's the equivalent of being Johnny Smith in *The Dead Zone,* coming out a decade-long coma and immediately being asked to moonwalk.

I feel as if I'm in an alternate reality, like El's 'Upside Down' in *Stranger Things*. Everything is the same, but different. In Fly Fishing Land, I hold my rod with my right hand. In Manu World, I hold it in my left. In Fly Fishing Land, I control the line with my left hand. In Manu World, it's the right. In Fly Fishing Land, the wrist is taken out of the equation. In Manu World, it makes your lure skip across the waves. Eventually, however, under Manu's patient tutelage, I begin to get there and soon enough, I'm getting fifty- and then sixty-foot casts out into the bay.

Switch his spinning road for a drumstick and the subtlety of Manu's wrist movement could make the cymbal on a drum kit vibrate as gently as if a butterfly were fluttering its wings next to it. *Moi*? I'm more Keith Moon: eyes popping out of my head, off my tits with a coal shovel full of angel dust up my hooter, going at a pair of metal dustbin lids with a pickaxe handle, yet the same bass still shoots out from among the rocks and goes for my lure.

I start at the bay end of the rocks, casting straight out in front of me. Manu is fishing to my left, banging out his lure into the mouth of the bay. Yes, you heard me correctly, I did say fishing, and he's soon into a very nice sea bass of around 2lb.

Now, I know that a fishing guide actually fishing while with a client would be an anathema to guides all over the UK, and I don't know if it's a French thing or Manu's own peculiarity, but whatever the case, I give my own inner Gallic shrug.

After all, there's plenty more bass in the sea.

We fish four bays in total that morning, but pick up all our fish in the wolverine's mouth. Manu has five sea bass ranging between 2–4lbs in size. The two I pick up are under a pound, looking like prehistoric, armour-plated versions of the first perch I ever caught, age ten, in the Grand Union Canal.

Completely overpowered by the gear we used, after the initial strike it is merely a case of reeling them in, but these are still among the hardest-earned fish I have ever caught.

The entrance to the hotel car park is blocked by a motorhome with a scooter attached to the back. Manu wins the exchange with the Italian driver by fifteen 'merdes,' two 'mother-fuckers' and a submission. Then, parking in a disabled bay, he breaks into a sneezing fit. He tells me that he always sneezes when he's hungry and he needs to get something to eat.

As I get out of the car, I ask him if he's ever been scared while fishing from the rocks. He says that the only time was when he was fishing for mackerel with a guy from Wales. The weather was getting worse and worse, and it was fifty-fifty as to whether or not they could continue. They were fishing with their backs to the sea when Manu heard a roaring sound, and he told the Welsh guy to crouch down and grab hold of the rock as hard as he could. He estimates that the wave that broke over them was twenty-feet high and had appeared from nowhere. They both took a soaking, but almost certainly avoided the drowning that would have occurred had they been swept off the rocks and out into the open sea.

Where I've been busy dodging virtual flaming barrels, Manu's been doing the real thing and saving his client's lives. Wild and unpredictable, yet offering excitement and sanctuary from the modern world, he couldn't be more Brittany if he dressed up as a schoolgirl and changed his surname to Spears.

Did I mention that I'm afraid of flying? That's another reason why we've been going to Brittany all these years. Ironically, as I'm trying to reduce my impact on the environment, my family are busy plotting a BA Baracus-style plan to get me on a plane. It might involve a spiked hamburger and maybe a Tarpon, but definitely not fishing with a 3WT.

I don't know when or if I'll ever go back to Brittany, but I hope it will stay as it is and the sea bass will always be there for Manu. Tragically, the impact of climate change says otherwise and I don't want to witness the inevitable decline of somewhere I love. Yet, as Manu wheel spins out of the car park, gives the finger to the driver of the motorhome and disappears in a cloud of sand, it isn't 'Goodbye' that I call out as I wave.

It's 'Au revoir.'

DURING

Head PTN * Grizzle Snake * Bead Head PTN with orange UV flash * Minkie Booby * Black Cri
Red Cheeked Black Cormorant * Booby Hopper Black * Black Tadpole * Black Bead PTN * Bla
PTN * Black Zonker * Plain Diawl Bach * Plain Cruncher * Black Zonker * Plain Diawl Bach * V
Nautilus * CDC Emerger * Nautilus * Weighted Nautilus * Plain Diawl Bach * Copper Bead PTN
Diawl Bach * Black Buzzer * Mark's Buzzer * Copper Bead Black Buzzer * Black Zonker *Black I
Red Holo Diawl Bach * Bibio * Bibio * Red-Arsed Hopper * Bibio * Red-Arsed Hopper * **Black**
* **Black Pennell**, Bibio * Kate McLaren * **Black Pennell** * Bibio * Kate McLaren * **Black Pennell**
* Kate McLaren * **Black Pennell** * Grizzle Snake * Red Holo JC Diawl Bach * JC Hot Head Diaw
Copper Head PTN with Orange Thorax * FAB Sunburst Blob * FAB Sunburst Blob * JC Hot Hea
Bach * Daddy LongLegs * Grizzle Snake * Black Bead PTN * Black Bead PTN * FAB Sunburst Blo
Holo Diawl Bach * Red Arsed Hopper * FAB Sunburst Blob * Black Cruncher * Red Holo Diaw
Cocktail Orange FAB * Black Cruncher * Red Arsed Hopper * **Black Pennell** * FAB Sunburst Blob
Cruncher * Red Holo Diawl Bach * Black Zonker * Red Holo Diawl Bach * Black Zonker * Grizzle
JC Minkie Booby * Mini Minkie Booby * JC Minkie Booby * Brown Minkie Booby * Black Zonker
Zonker * Buoyant Crayfish * PTN Black Bead * Nautilus * Silver Minkie Booby * Dress Bead Blo
* Black Bead Grey Boy Buzzer * Black Diawl Bach * Nautilus * FAB Sunburst Blob * JC Minkie
Red Booby * Grizzle Snake * Plain Diawl Bach * JC Hot Head Diawl Bach * Pink Snake * Black Z
Mark's Buzzer * Sunburst FAB * Red Holo Diawl Bach and Black Shipman's * Coch-Y-Bonddu *
Fritz PTN * Natural Hot Spot Tungsten PTN * Black Cruncher Red Holo Cheek * Green Holo Dia
* Black Shipman's * Black Bead PTN * Grizzle Snake * Micro Blue Flash Damsel * Green Hol
Bach * Black Shipman's * Red Holo Diawl Bach * Booby Hopper * Black Shipman's * Red Ho
Bach * Green Holo Diawl Bach * Booby Damsel * Black Popper Hopper * Red-Arsed Black H
Black Pennell * CDC Elk * **Black Pennell** * Yellow Tailed Bibio * CDC Elk * White Arse Kate Mc
White Arse Kate McLaren * Kate McLaren Muddler * **Black Pennell** * **Black Pennell** * Captain
* **Black Pennell** * Black Zonker * White Arsed Kate McLaren * Captain Peacock * Black Bea
Silver Minkie Booby * Black Bead PTN * Black Diawl Bach * Pink Snake * Black UV Buzzer * Pink
Grizzle Snake * Sunburst FAB * Tequila Blob * White Humungous * Black Zonker * Olive Zonker
Zonker * Olive Zonker * Mini Blob Booby Cocktail Coral * Cocktail Orange FAB * Cocktail Oran
* Jelly Tequila FAB *Cocktail Orange FAB * Sunburst FAB * Cocktail Orange FAB * Jelly Tequil
Grizzle Snake * Olive Zonker * Cocktail Orange FAB * Jelly Tequila FAB * Olive Snake * Blac
*Pink Snake * Grizzle Snake * Black Snake * Jelly Tequila FAB * Bloodworm * Red Holo
* Black Bead PTN * Black Bead PTN * Gold Ribbed Hare's Ear * Green Montana * JC Red Hol
Bach * Hot Head Cruncher * Sunburst FAB * Black Cruncher * Traffic Light Buzzer * Black Be
* **Black Pennell** * Black Cruncher with Red Holo Cheeks * Black Cruncher * Gold Head PTN *
Holo Diawl Bach * **Black Pennell** * Hot Head Captain Peacock * Gold head PTN * Black Cr
* Black Cruncher with Silver Thorax * **Black Pennell** * Booby Hopper * Grizzle Snake * **Black Pe**
Kate McLaren * Claret Shipman's * Cocktail Orange FAB * Pretender * Hutch's Pennell * Leggy
Pretender * Hutch's Pennell * Leggy Pretender * Captain Peacock * Nautilus * Nautilus * Foam
* **Black Pennell** * Damsel * Red Arse Kate * Hare's Ear Sedgehog * Wickhams Fancy * Yellow Ta
* **Black Pennell** * Bibio Hopper * Wickhams Fancy * Yellow Tail Bibio * **Black Pennell** * Wi
Fancy * Yellow Tail Bibio * **Black Pennell** * Wickhams Fancy * Yellow tail Bibio * **Black Pennel**
Elk and Wickhams Fancy * Pretender * Leggy Pretender * Black Zonker * Leggy Pretender * Wh
Kate McLaren * Leggy Bibio * **Black Pennell** * Black Zonker * Nautilus* Nautilus * Cocktail Oran
* Mini Blob Booby Coral * Cocktail Orange FAB * Cocktail Orange FAB * Sunburst FAB * Grizzle

from the wind yielded as much as a swirl at our flies. It's looking like one of those days when the fickle fishing finger of fate taps you on the shoulder and whispers,: 'It ain't your night, kid,' and a one-way ticket to Blanksville beckons. My eyes are inextricably drawn to the ridge in the far distance and I wonder if Tweedle Dia and Tweddle Dafydd are faring any better than us.

Our blank is saved by a chance encounter with Welsh fishing legends George Barron and Gayle Marsh. In one of those weird coincidences, we've recently been exchanging emails about Aberystwyth Angling's waters, which I fished a few weeks ago. George tells us that Egnant hasn't been fishing well all year and puts us on to some fish on Llyn Hir, where he and Gayle had been earlier. Llyn Hir is a long, narrow lake, lying between Llyn Egnant and Llyn Teifi and it's only a short walk across a bog from where we've moved our cars to.

There are fewer fish in Llyn Hir, but they're bigger and I take a nice brownie of around a pound in the evening. George also gives me the white-arsed Kate McLaren that catches it, hard up against a sheer rock face. Before he leaves, I can't help asking about the quad twins and the lake beyond the ridge. George knows the boys, they're good fisherman, but when last seen, they were heading in completely the wrong direction.

Neither George nor Gayle have ever fished there.

Being someone whose idea of a good time is sitting by themselves in a darkened room writing nonsense or staring at water for hours on end, I've coped pretty well with the lockdown and working from home for the last six months. What I've coped less well with is having the places I go to escape being overrun by the people I'm desperately trying to get away from. Like white wine and lager, some things just shouldn't mix, and fly fishing and the general public are two of them. My own personal relationship with the non-fly fishing fraternity was defined early on by Brockwell Park's answer to Oscar Wilde yelling, 'Oi, paedo! Stop fishing for kids!' at me, while I was practising my casting on the grass by the swings.

It was an amicable split. I agreed to go my own way, which happened to be as far away from theirs as possible. It all worked well until the pandemic hit, when with shopping villages, chain restaurants and package holidays unavailable, the Covidiots suddenly started banging on the gates of my happy places. MGFSLX got poached, the Barrows became Daytona Beach for the NOS set and every river with a fishy-looking pool within a twenty-mile radius of my home became a beach. This wouldn't necessarily have been a bad thing if their exposure to the countryside had led to a deeper connection with nature, and a greater awareness of the threats it faces from climate change, pollution and plastic. However, all it highlighted was that along with Father Christmas, the Easter Bunny and Britannia once again ruling the waves post-Brexit, there also seems to be a shared belief among the masses of a magical fucking fairy that makes wet wipes, cans of cider, bags of dog shit, abandoned tents and disposable BBQs disappear.

My jaunt with Steve M to the Teifi Pools was the latest in a series of road trips over the summer and autumn, seeking solitude among the hill lakes of mid-Wales while chasing wild brown trout in remote places I can't pronounce. I've found a few fish, but my happy place has been harder to locate.

The trip to the aforementioned Aberystwyth Angling's waters was an abject failure. The first lake I fished had a crew of thirty working on the dam, and the second and third were either side of a crossroads that turned out to be a spaghetti junction for mountain bikers, camper vans and day trippers. The fourth was surrounded on three sides by a hamlet and last seen as a body dump site in an episode of *Hinterland.*

As good a time as it's been fishing with Steve M, there's that familiar feeling of an itch I've failed to scratch. I can't help but wonder if my best chance of finding the solitude I crave, and one of those mythical 'red letter' days where the trout are willing and I'm able, lies on the other side of that ridge.

And anyway, I'm a sucker for a secret lake story.

When I get home, I set up a media alert for 'quad bike', 'dead' and 'Teifi Pools,' and then set about finding what I can on the lake beyond the ridge. The first thing I learn is its name, Llyn Gynon. It's shaped like a ghost wearing a sheet, lying on its side with the head pointing west. The lake lies between two hills, Crug Gynon and Ban-Y-Lyn, with Nant Brwynog emerging from its spectral tail into Claaerwen Reservoir, and Nant Gwinau running down towards Llyn Egnant to the North, before vanishing into a bog. The second thing I learn is that it's only an hour's walk from Llyn Egnant. There are no reports online from anyone who has fished it, so I email George Barron to see if he can put me in touch with the *Blewog Bikers.*

Apparently, they made it home in one piece. George said they found fish on one side of the lake, and it was 'a fish a chuck.' He signs off with 'Fisherman's tales.'

Watching *YouTube*, the concept of wild camping seemed a natural way to extend my trips up to Wales to overnight, reducing the need for blatting up the A470 at dawn, and avoiding the boy racers recreating *Project Gotham Racing* on Merthyr Tydfil's dual carriageways at night. In reality, the combination of confinement, the smell of the waterproof lining and unnatural positioning of sleeping in a bivvy bag left me feeling like I was recreating one of the BTK's outdoor bondage selfies. And then there's the rain. In my two overnight trips to Wales so far, I've spent the sum total of one hour and thirty-seven minutes sleeping outside. On my Aberystwyth trip, a downpour of biblical proportions meant that I never even made it into my bivvy bag. The second trip, to the Teifi Pools with Steve M, I at least made it into my bivvy bag before the rain started. It then got progressively heavier until it became similar to going through a car wash in a femdom, while having frozen peas fired at you from an air compressor. I was then faced with the classic rock and hard place scenario of deciding whether to stay in my bivvy bag getting soaked by the rain pouring in through the opening, or to get soaked making a mad dash in my pants and wellies for the car. I briefly considered wriggling along the ground from my camping spot by the lakeside to my car, like a giant red maggot, but I didn't want to freak Steve M into thinking he'd stumbled into a Welsh reboot of *Tremors*.

Hoping that it's going to be third time lucky on my trip to Llyn Gynon, I've spent the last two weeks fastidiously studying the weather forecast for back-to-back dry days. The only problem is, I completely overlooked the wind speed. On a lowland reservoir, a 13mph ENE is exactly what it says on the tin. At 1,300ft, the same 13mph ENE is gusting to 40mph.

I'm parked next to the dam on Llyn Egnant and my car is vibrating. If I'd parked side-on to the wind, I think it'd be in real danger of being blown over. It's 5.30pm and this is my second trip up to the Teifi Pools today. It was recycling day in Tregaron, and on the way up this morning, I was slaloming around green plastic boxes in a dust cloud of yoghurt pots and ready meal containers. Higher up, the wind was blowing the length of all six Teifi Pools, turning them into inland seas. With the pools unfishable and still another 600ft to climb in a wind that I can hardly stand up in, I didn't fancy the odds of finding a sheltered bay I could fish. Instead, I dropped down to the other side of the valley and fished Llyn Berwyn, a small, shallow lake in a pine forest, twenty minutes' drive east of Tregaron.

I had hoped that the wind would have dropped by now, but it hasn't. If anything, it's even stronger. I need to hole-up somewhere for the night, hope the wind drops and head for Llyn Gynon in the morning, but where? It's too windy to wild camp and I'd rather bunk-up with BTK in his El Dorado Correctional Facility prison cell than face another night sleeping in the front passenger seat of my car. I'd heard there's a bothy across the other side of the narrow, single-lane road that is the only way in and out from the Teifi Pools, but due to my pathological fear of sharing confined spaces with strangers, I'm hesitant. It's not that they might be serial killers or Tottenham fans, or both, it's that I'm incapable of feigning interest in someone or something I'm not interested in, and subsequently having to extricate myself from a socially awkward situation. There's only so many times I can play the 'autistic spectrum' card.

I drive back to the road and abandon my car in a passing bay, which, according to Google Maps, should be directly opposite the bothy, and as I follow a farm track down into a valley, I'm pleasantly surprised. I thought bothies were tiny mountainside shelters consisting of loose stone walls and corrugated roofs. What awaits me is a two-storey slate-grey farmhouse, complete with an outhouse and a stream running out the front. Standing outside, trying to get a fire going in a metal pot, are Lancashire's answer to Jesse and Chester. Jesse is bearded, with a gamer's pallor and physique to match. He's wearing knee-length board shorts, a baggy black T-shirt and ankle socks with no shoes. Chester is wearing a V-neck jumper with a pair of joggers. His head is shaved, and the closeness of his eyes, along with his height, would've earned him the nickname

'Lofty' in a '70s sitcom. It takes them more than an hour to get the fire going and the water boiled, which they promptly spill before they can get it into a mug. They then nearly give us all carbon monoxide poisoning while transferring the burning embers from the pot into the Bothy's stove, filling the ground floor with black smoke. God only knows what they think of a southern fly fishing ponce like me; probably a cross between JR Hartley and Uncle Monty, armed with a stash of Rohypnol for an act of midnight burglary, as irrelevant and anachronistic to them as a Betamax video.

The bothy is better equipped than some of the holiday homes I've stayed in. The wooden benches along the wall to the right of the door are wide enough to sleep on, there's a dining room with a table where a wood-burning stove squats in the corner, a kitchen with a sink and running water, and a better assortment of condiments than I've got at home. Battery-powered fairy lights and empty silver candle holders attest to the fact that there's no electricity or light inside once the sun goes down. It's got that evocative smoke-filled, candle soot-stained vibe of an early-twentieth century pub, and I'm half expecting to see the *Peaky Blinders* conspiring in the corner.

It turns out that Jesse and Chester are refugees from their local lockdown. They've driven down in a car that has only three gears, none of which are reverse. To make the car go backwards, they have to engage in a Fred Flintstone-type manoeuvre by opening the driver's door, putting a foot on the floor and pushing backwards. Jesse works at an IT call centre. He's recently returned from Spain, where he spent the entire lockdown confined to his flat. It's clear that being locked down in a former fascist state with police drones flying overhead and SWAT teams descending on you the second you set foot outside was no picnic. Every time I ask a question about the lockdown in

the far bank. Although the water is the same depth for the first ten feet, it quickly deepens and I rise my first fish of the day, quickly followed by my first hook-up. It's a small brownie, and the strength of the wind, combined with the weight of the rod, causes a lack of feeling similar to that experienced by Stormy Daniels while on her way to earning $130,000.

'Is it on?... '

'Is it off?... '

'Where is it? ...'

'Is it in the net? ...'

'Are you sure? ...'

It turns out it isn't, but my frustration at failing to pop my Gynon cherry is tempered by my relief at finally finding fish. They are hitting the flies as soon as they touch the water. Instead of trying to cast as far as I can across the face of the wind, I concentrate on casting shorter, turning my flies over and ensuring they land properly on the water. I continue to rise and hook fish, but none of them make it into the net.

The takes dry up as I reach a sheltered bay that marks the start of the downwind shore. From there, I head back up to the top of the bank and re-fish the area I'd just covered with a small peacock lure with an orange hothead. Different fly, same story. Most upland lakes fall into two categories: lots of small fish or a small number of bigger ones. It looks like Llyn Gynon falls into the former category. In going with the 7wt to cope with the wind, I'm massively over-gunned and finally have to admit the folly of bringing a Death Star to a kittens' play fight.

Luckily, unlike Loris Karius in the 2018 Champions League Final, there aren't 60,000 people, plus a worldwide TV audience of millions, on hand to witness my ineptitude. I'm an hour's walk away from my car, which is a twenty-minute drive from civilisation. I have no mobile signal and Google Maps has

just uttered the words I have been longing to hear since I came
to Wales:

'GPS lost.'

I am utterly alone, on my tod, Gideon, Billy No Mates,
Bill Bixby at the end of every episode of The Incredible Hulk TV
show, and, fish or no fish, I am loving it. It's just me in a green
desert with a sprinkling of sheep, The Lonely Man Theme tinkling
in my head and not a Covidiot in sight.

Shibby!

There's a brief moment of panic on my way back to the car. It's
either down to lack of sleep, exhaustion or light-headedness
from being in the sun all day, but instead of following the quad
bike tracks east, I head north in a much straighter direction
than when I came. Soon, even the sheep trails have been
swallowed up by the marsh grass, and I find myself stumbling
over tussocks and crossing a deep stream bed carved into the
peat. I have a reasonably decent compass in my head, and
whether on foot or in a car, I always try to take note of features
on my way somewhere, to help me find my way back. None of
this looks familiar to me, and as I top the latest rise, there's
no sign of Llyn Egnant. I finally realise that I'm heading too
straight and begin pushing east, but it's tough going with no
sheep tracks to follow, and I can feel myself becoming more
tired with each step. Then, rounding a crescent-shaped ridge, I
see a metal gate that I climbed over on my way to the lake, and
I know I am on my way home.

With Llyn Egnant and my car parked by the dam in
sight, I can finally relax, and like a horse who can smell home,
I find myself speeding up. Going downhill also helps and I soon
reach the top of the dam. Traditionally, before driving home,
I'll grab an hour's kip in my car, and then brew a strong coffee

to wake myself for the journey home. I'm about to step onto the dam when I notice the wave on Llyn Egnant. The two most prominent features of Llyn Egnant are the rounded tump that me and Steve M parked on a lifetime ago, and a 30ft-high rock outcrop that emerges from the black peat bank like a half-submerged leviathan. The wind is blowing straight down the reservoir onto the dam, creating a perfect wind lane on the sheltered side of Big Bad Barry's head. The rods are in their tubes strapped to my backpack and all my tackle is inside, so the question is, can I really be arsed to tackle-up again in the hope there's a fish lurking there that will break my blank?

Does shit-housery course through Sergio Ramos's veins?

Learning from my mistakes on Llyn Gynon, I string up my 5wt with a Kelly Green intermediate. Although lighter, the lower-profile line cuts through the side wind with ease, and second cast, my Black Pennell is whacked the instant the flies touch the water. There's no chance of not feeling connected with this fish; it's like I've licked my finger and shoved it in an 240v electricity socket. It feels bigger than any wild brownie I've ever come into contact with; it bores deep and I play it hard. This time, I don't mess around with the net and beach it on the black peat bank. It's 17" long, fat as a hog, with a tail you could dig your own grave with, and it weighs over 2lbs.

I'm left experiencing what Chester would refer to as a state of 'sense memory stimulated perception altered consciousness memory retrieval.' The irony of catching my best wild brownie to date a hundred yards from my car, after walking for more than two hours across rough ground and climbing a combined elevation of 1,200ft, is not lost on me. However, at this precise moment in time, my 'give-a-shit-ometer,' which has climate change at one end and the Kardashians at the other, is currently registering this fact at less than Donald Trump's feelings.

As I come back down to earth I become aware of what looks like the cast of *The Real Housewives of Cheshire* emerging from a pair of matching black BMW X5s and making their way noisily around the track on the opposite side of the reservoir to me. The kids and dads scramble down the bank and hurl rocks into the water, like Louis Vuitton trebuchets. A teenage girl, silhouetted by the setting sun, climbs up onto the dam wall and takes a picture of me fishing.

#Paedo #FishingforKids

The completion of the quest is marked by what Vogler calls the 'Return with the elixir.' In layman's terms, it's what I say to my daughter after bizarrely binge-watching the latest episode of '80s sitcom *Fuller House* on *Netflix*.

'Did they learn something and do they love each other?'

My own quest is complete. After refusing the call, I met with mentors before crossing the threshold, exploring my special world and, as ever, making friends and enemies in equal measure. After approaching my innermost cave, facing my greatest challenge and experiencing fishing death and rebirth, I have followed the road back to the ordinary world and my ultimate resurrection.

While not as earth-shattering as Perceval's realisation after finding the Holy Grail in John Boorman's *Excalibur* – that the king and the land are one – I realise that the most difficult thing isn't going up into the mountains.

It's coming back down again.

Cue: O Fortuna.

All that's separating me from the Land of the Covidiots

is 250ft of Victorian dam. A strong coffee and a kip can wait.
I think I'll just stay here a little while longer.

No Más

This is madness. My windscreen wipers can't keep up with the rain hammering down in the pre-dawn darkness. Overtaking a car transporter loaded with showroom-ready BMWs is a game of chicken. I count five Mississippis before the spray obscuring my view of the M4 clears. I should ease off, tuck in behind the HGVs in the slow lane and join the convoy of work vans and shift workers, but I can't. It's like I'm riding the fruits of Jeff Bezos' silver penis vanity project, slingshotting the Earth, accelerating to achieve escape velocity and break free from the gravitational pull of my non-fishing life.

I'm leaving behind Kent variants, three-tiered alert levels and all the corona-comms I'm going to have to write – until they become specks in my rear view mirror, like the headlights from the highway maintenance truck. I raise my travel mug to Richey Manic as I race over the Severn Estuary and don't slow down until I turn off the A449 at Raglan, where a first glimpse of the Black Mountains confirms entry into my new orbit.

It's late October and I'm on a two-day fishing trip to Clywedog Reservoir in Powys. With Wales entering a firebreak lockdown at the end of the week, it's my last trip of the season. There's not a breath of wind in the bay to the left of the jetty; the twenty or so boats I'm sharing the reservoir with are motionless and pointing in every direction. It's like being in a *Strictly* dance routine choreographed by Alexi Sayle's Egbert and Bill. The fish are hard on buzzers and rising indiscriminately. I'm fishing a floating line with size-sixteen black CDC buzzers, as prescribed by some of the Welsh boys I've been in contact with on *Facebook* in the run-up to the trip. Yet two hours' fishing has seen a single rainbow trout nudge my point fly.

I head into the bottleneck by the cages. This is where the ranger recommended that I fish, before I got distracted by the rising fish in Eblid. *Strictly* has become Rome in rush hour. Casting at a rising fish tight up against the rock face, a boat tries to squeeze through the narrow gap between me and the bank. I wave him away and he gives me the thumbs up. It's all good-natured.

For me, fly fishing is an act of seduction between trout and angler. Some days, it requires the subtlety of Faye Dunaway and Steve McQueen exchanging smouldering non-verbals over a chess board, while others it takes the equivalent of flashing your headlights in Toghill car park. Having gone through my fly box, and with my flashing headlights now issuing an SOS rather than attracting punters, I take the glory hole option and tie on a six-inch pink snake.

The Shepherd's Hut is a fifteen-minute drive from Clywedog, and having spent a total of 96 minutes in a bivvy bag on my previous three attempts at overnighting in the Welsh mountains, I've decided to treat myself. I'm sitting in front of the fire pit, toasting the complimentary bag of pink-and-white Haribo Chamallows, while my sling pack, yellow fishing jacket and waterproof trousers hang drying from the tiki bar awning over the stainless-steel outdoor sink and industrial three-burner BBQ.

8.30am. I text the owner, Suzi, about check-out times. She tells me they've got no one arriving today, so I can stay as long as I want. I put a cushion on the reclining garden chair and sit with a coffee in my hand, gazing across the meadow to where three valleys intersect beyond. I'm feeling slightly naughty, as if I've bunked off school or chucked a sicky, when an RAF Typhoon fighter jet passes in front of me at eye level. Over the next couple of hours, I'm treated to the kind of fly-past usually reserved for dead royals or Middle-Eastern dictators, featuring another Typhoon, a Hawk T-2 and a grey C130-J bringing up the rear, like a couch potato running their first 10k.

Not fishing never felt so good.

The 20lbs-plus carp once chased by a teenage Chris Yates are as long gone as my Uncle Vernon's menswear shop on Llandrindod Wells's high street. They're not even a memory to the middle-aged guy fishing from a wooden platform. He tells me the lake was drained a number of years ago to put aerators in and restocked. He's fishing with PVA bags and jokes about 'carp tax' and being out-fished by his twenty-year-old son sat on the next peg down.

The only monsters here now are the red dragon pedalos. In the lakeside cafe I'm sitting outside, their terrestrial offspring roars and guffs clouds of dry ice, while a skeleton hillbilly sits above the plastic jars of rosy apples and pineapple rock playing Duelling Banjos. They're the Statue of Liberty to my time-travelling Charlton Heston living in a world ruled by chimps, but I resist the temptation to sink to my knees, pound the asphalt and scream, 'God damn you all to hell!'. Although in my case, it's more a question of aesthetics rather than the realisation of the horrors that we as human beings are capable of inflicting on one another.

As ever, when returning to a childhood haunt,

everything seems smaller and more crowded. None more so than the picnic area out of town by the River Ithon. I remember the feeling of seemingly having the whole place to ourselves when spending our summer holidays at the Kendrick's farmhouse a couple of miles upstream. Today, I'm sharing it with cyclists, walkers, families and a mother and daughter leading a brown-and-white horse into the forest by its reins.

A downed beech tree is wedged lengthwise between the struts of the wooden foot bridge, collecting white foam and bleached branches. It's from here that I first cast a rod and watched incredulously as swarms of minnows ignored the silver foil wrapped around my size-ten hook. In contrast to the lake and town centre feeling like Legoland, I'm reassuringly dwarfed by the hill towering over me, with the remains of Cefnllys Castle at its peak. I turn right and make my way along a bank shaded by the gnarled trunks and twisted branches of ancient hawthorn trees, past the rapids that were always too swift for our stick floats. The barbed wire fence on the edge of the floodplain that marks the boundary is flattened and choked by a dried mat of weed. I take it as an invitation to press on. When the river cuts into the base of the hill, I'm forced to climb, following a sheep trail cut into the earth that grows narrower as it rises, until it suddenly vanishes and I find myself suspended forty feet above the river, with nothing below me but rocks and water.

I've no choice other than to jump across the abyss and them I'm heading down to where our crossing point used to be. It's where one summer I found a dying salmon, exhausted from spawning, gasping between the stepping stones. Opposite is the undercut bank where, after bringing maggots with me for the first time on holiday, I watched the same minnows that ignored the tin foil devour them like mini piranhas, resulting in previously unthinkable catches.

I reach the longer, deeper stretch of the river, where the flow slows to a crawl. It's where we used to swim until we discovered it was home to a giant pike, as unexpected, exotic and dangerous to us as any great white shark. Ten more steps brings me to where I caught my first brown trout, improbably, on the first day of the year in freezing, torrential rain, using a worm floated in water that was the colour and consistency of an Oreo Freakshake.

The Kendrick's white-washed farmhouse may have grown a glass-fronted extension, and the two derelict barns converted into holiday lets, but the trees we'd climb to spot chub and freeline floating crust under its roots on the current, are still the same. Although I never fly fished on the River Ithon, it's where my love of sight-fishing and casting at feeding fish on the surface first developed, leading to the random purchase of a fly fishing kit for another holiday, this time in the Limousin, some twenty years later.

The A420 and Eddie Cochran beckons for the final leg of my dead rockers' roadshow. I'm in no hurry, though. On my way home, I might stop and look over the side of the Glanusk Estate's towered bridge. Getting a special fried rice from the Chinese take-away in Crickhowell would be nice. A freshly-pulled pint even better.

And sure as a pink snake will always save a blank, the pubs will reopen. When they do, I'll raise my first pint to Gouldy, Eddie, Kurt, Richey, red dragon pedalos and banjo-playing hillbilly skeletons.

THE DIPPING

CERTIFICATE

X

ADULTS ONLY

The Werewolf in the Living Room

It's rooted in my most vivid childhood memory. I'm six years old, eating fish fingers and chips in the dining room. The glass doors that separate the dining room from the living room are open, and I have an unobstructed view of the Sony Trinitron that sits at eye-level in the white Habitat wall unit. I'm vaguely aware that something unusual is happening on screen. There's a darkened staircase, a shadow descending and laboured breathing. Something sinister is prowling through a house. Then, at the exact moment I look up from my fish fingers, there's a close-up of the face of a werewolf looking straight back at me through a gap in a bookcase.

Our eyes lock, mine widening by the millisecond, the werewolf's wild and bloodshot. I scream. Chips fly. My mum comes running. I'm in tears. Inconsolable. Scared shitless; too afraid to close my eyes and go to sleep for the next two weeks.

A lifelong pathological fear of the dark or, more specifically, what might lurk there, is born. Anything with a hairy face holds a particular terror: *Planet of the Apes*, the robot Big Foot in *The Six Million Dollar Man*, Dave Lee Travis and, of course, werewolves. Fuelled by the unique layout of our upside down house, with the bedrooms on the ground floor, the Ladder in *Jacob's Ladder* had nothing on my nightmares: watching my mum descend the stairs and seeing a werewolf waiting for her out-of-sight at the bottom, but being too terrified to shout out a warning and watching her being eaten alive; one of the gorilla soldiers from *Planet of the Apes* climbing in through the bedroom window and carrying me away; and Nandi bears cracking open my skull and eating my brains. Too scared to make my way down the darkened hallway to my parents' bedroom, my only defence was singing the theme tune to *The Pink Panther Show* in an attempt to get back to my happy place.

The offending show was *Nationwide*, a forerunner to *The One Show*, hosted by a cuddly Frank Bough in his pre-S&M dungeon expose days. It was a bizarre mix of current affairs, celebrity profiles and British eccentricity. Any given episode could see an in-depth interview with the leader of the SDP (ask your parents) sitting alongside a report from the Durham Leek Show, vox pops on subjects such as the UK switching from miles to kilometres with various Mrs Brady look-a-likes, Richard Stilgoe showing viewers how to rewire a fuse and, apparently, live werewolves stalking suburban semis

It was on at 6pm on a school night. Welcome to the '70s, kids.

Given my pathological fear of the dark, the idea of solo wild camping in a bivvy bag in the Cambrian Mountains might seem like a weird choice. Truth is, as ever, I haven't thought things all the way through. On my first attempt at solo wild camping, during a two-day road trip taking in five of Aberystwyth Angling's waters, my main concern isn't what happens after the sun sets. Instead, it's that my choice of camping spot on the shore of Llyn Syfydrin isn't isolated enough for me to have one of what chef Jose Andreas calls, in an episode of *Parts Unknown*, his 'moments of solitude.'

Judging by the number of stone rings with blackened embers in the middle, the patch of grass I'm sitting on as I eat a Tesco mozzarella and tomato pasta with chilli sauce straight from the saucepan, looks like it's a regular camping spot for visitors. There are also motocross tracks running up the grass hillock behind me, and the parking area is littered with bottles, cans and empty fast-food containers, looking exactly like the kind of teenage make-out spot where the Zodiac Killer earned his chops.

My plan is to fish the evening rise while my three cans of Evil Juice cool in the lake, and then climb inside my bivvy bag. Given how well-used the camping area looks, I know that everyone with a rod in their car who has parked here has probably had a chuck from the car park shore. I walk back up along the levee with the stone track running down it, before fishing my way back down towards the camping area. Unusually for me, I'm fishing dries with a single CDC Elk on the point. I'd fished Craig y Pistyll earlier, and, after going fishless before lunch with traditional wets, I put on a CDC Elk when I saw trout rising out in the middle. Casting out beneath a cliff face over a bed of pond weed, the fish came blind to it before the rain rolled in again and killed the briefest of brief rises.

They're not so keen on the CDC Elk at Syfydrin, but I fluke my first brownie of the evening, stripping it in to recast. I add a Black Pennell on the dropper and take a second fish with huge bug eyes, not unlike mine that night I saw the *Nationwide* werewolf. Meanwhile, things begin to liven up at the lakeside, as a couple of kids in a VW transporter van roll down the track and park beside my car. Then, as I reach the campsite, a guy on a touring bike pulls up.

The light is fading fast and the splash of rising fish is getting louder. Despite my previous misgivings, I have a few casts from the campsite shore, banging out a long cast from a stony bay that looks like a favourite paddling spot for day trippers. A big trout slashes at the CDC and misses, but it comes back for seconds and my line goes solid. I only become aware of the two kids from the transporter van standing behind me as I admire a brownie that weighs more than a pound in my landing net. Their collie dog gives the brown trout a lick before I slip it back. They've come down from Manchester; the lad fishes for carp and asks lots of good questions about fly fishing. He's got a spinning rod with him and they move down the shore for an exploratory cast or two.

The wind has picked up and blows onto the car park shore. It's getting too dark to see. I take a final fish on the Pennell and then head back to the camping area. When the guy on the touring bike asks if you can camp by the lake, I scare him off by responding to his question as if I was Joe Pesci in *Goodfellas*, being told by Ray Liotta that he was funny.

'What do you mean, "can I camp here?" Do I look like Ray fucking Mears to you?'

I'm less bothered by the kids, as they soon retire to the comfort of their van, leaving me with the entire camping spot to myself. When they do finally drive off, the relief I feel is more to do with no longer feeling like a weird uncle, rather than finally being on my own.

I sit in my chair, crack open a can of Evil Juice and read Amy Lawrence's *Invincible* on my Kindle for an hour. The waves I'm getting from my choice of camping spot are definitely more Oddball than Moriarty, then just as I'm about to get into my bivvy bag, it starts raining.

I grab my bivvy bag and sleeping bag and run for the car. I read for another hour, hoping the rain will eventually stop, but it doesn't. It gets heavier and heavier. After locking the doors, I recline the passenger seat as far back as it will go, which turns out to be 60° shy of the 180° I was hoping for, and get into my sleeping bag.

A red light that I've never noticed before pulses on the dashboard.

And so I chased the horror. In the '70s, I didn't have to look far, when in between the likes of the *Crackerjack* and *Magic Roundabout*, I could watch *Children of the Stones* and *Shadows*. As well as werewolves on tea-time current affairs shows, on a weekday I could see *Sapphire and Steele* at 7pm, *The Omega Factor* at 8pm and, on Saturday nights, *Hammer House of Horror* at 9pm, followed by the horror double bills on BBC 2. Anything featuring werewolves held a particular terror for me, but from Henry Hull to Lon Chaney Jr to Oliver Reed to David Naughton, I forced myself to sit through every transformation from man to the source of my darkest nightmares.

It's the *Hammer House of Horror* that I'm thinking about when I sit bolt upright just before 2am. Surprisingly, it's not *The Children of the Full Moon* episode, but *The Two Faces of Evil*. It's the rain hammering on the roof of the car that does it, along with the fact that the windows are so thick with condensation, I can't see outside.

My eyes catch the empty backseat in the rear-view mirror. I strain to hear the crunching of stones beneath someone's boots as they walk around the car, imagining the back door opening and feeling the car sink under the weight of them sitting down on the backseat wearing a yellow oil slicker and matching hat. Their head is tipped forward, so that the upturned collar of their raincoat and hat obscures their face. Finally, they raise their head just enough to expose my own face looking back at me, and a grin exposing a row of rotten stumps for teeth.

I jerk awake and look at the clock. Eleven minutes have

passed. I have the fear – bad. Beyond having a couple of beers, ensuring my reading material gave nothing for my inner chimp to spontaneously combust on and definitely not thinking about the person who drowned in Llyn Syfydrin almost seven years to the day I'm camping here, I hadn't given much thought as to how to deal with this situation. When it comes to making potentially life-changing decisions, I'm the equivalent of Franz Reichelt, who infamously leapt to his death from the Eiffel Tower in 1912 while testing a flying parachute suit. Franz was very thorough when it came to constructing a series of sturdy makeshift steps out of the chairs and tables from the floor of the Eiffel Tower's first deck up onto the balustrade. But when it came to what would happen after he leapt... not so thorough. Swap my bivvy bag for Franz's batsuit and I realise there's a piece of exquisitely-manicured Parisian lawn rapidly rushing up towards me at 120mph.

All I know is that I want to get the fuck out of Dodge. From here, my night descends into a series of horror film cliches where I find myself doing everything I'm usually yelling at the protagonists not to do. First, realising my camping chair and cooking pots are still by the side of the lake, I leave the sanctuary of my car and throw them into the boot, hopefully missing my 5wt, which rather optimistically, given my current state of blind panic, I hadn't bothered to put back in its tube, as I was intending to have a fish at first light. Next, finding the stone track on top of the levee blocked by a gate, my mind calculates exactly when I'm going to get eviscerated by whatever is lurking in the pine forest bordering the levee.

Will it be as I step out of the car? I wonder. *As I close the distance between me and the gate? As I fumble with the latch? As I walk back to the car with my back to the forest on the other side of the gate? As I put my hand on the door handle, inches from sanctuary?*

I picture the POV shot of something watching me from between the trees; moving, prowling, coming closer. I can feel hot, fetid breath on my neck...

Driving down from the mountains, my brain is still somewhere between being asleep and awake. The road is flooded. The lanes are a maze. I'm a mess. I can't remember the theme tune to *The Pink Panther Show* and I don't even know if I'm heading in the right direction. Then I drive over the cattle grid with the sign for Ponterwyd and see the lights of a cottage ahead. I pull into a lay-by beneath some trees. Large drops of rain fall from the branches onto the roof of my car, in time to the *boom! boom! boom!* of the vein pulsing in my neck. There's a fence made of corrugated iron sheets to my left. Behind me is a pair of double garages and a plastic yellow grit bin. I'm just glad to be near a light and close to people again. At some point, I fall asleep for what feels like all of ten minutes before the dawn chorus starts.

From here, the trip becomes a bust, as I drive back up into the mountains and blank at Llyn Blaenmelindwr and Rhosgoch. Heavy black clouds are gathering over the Irish Sea, and an old boy fishing ahead of me on Llyn Rhosgoch tells me there's a big storm rolling in tomorrow. I take another drenching while running back to the car, and on my way to fish Llyn yr Oerfa, I stop off at the tourist centre to check the forecast, getting confirmation that tomorrow will see torrential rain and 40mph-plus winds from 7am.

Shuddering like a shitting dog at the thought of spending a second sleepless night in my passenger seat, and after a further blank at Llyn Oerfa, fish and chips in Rhayader is looking more and more appealing.

The thud of my boot closing sounds very much like the noise Franz Reichelt made hitting the frozen ground after plunging 187 feet from the first deck of the Eiffel Tower.

A combination of conditions, companionship and comfort allows my werewolf in the living room to remain undisturbed throughout the rest of the season. The weather curtails any attempt of spending the night in my bivvy bag on my two trips to the Teifi Pools, while the company of Steve M, Chester and Jessie ensures that the night terrors are mostly kept at bay. I am woken in the early hours by something furry, with teeth and claws, on my final trip of the season to Clywedog Reservoir, but that's just a parkouring squirrel on the roof of the Shepherd's Hut.

For the new season, I invest in a one-man tent to take conditions out of the equation, and I try not to think of all the horror films involving lone campers. From this point onward, my preparation is all about planning for the moment where I climb inside my sleeping bag, zip up my tent flaps and put a silver cap in the hairy ass of my werewolf in the living room. I await the nod from George Barron that things have warmed up enough for the brown trout to start feeding.

My first trip up into the Cambrian Mountains isn't until mid-May, a day trip to Craig Goch with Steve M. It's cold and it pisses down all day, plus the estate patrols are notoriously quick to move on anyone who looks like they might be wild camping, so my tent stays at home.

The cold weather continues and even the legendary rises at the Barrows are subdued affairs confined to twenty-foot lengths of the causeway, sheltered from the freezing wind blowing straight in off the Bristol Channel. I plan a series of trips into the mountains based on long-range forecasts, only to cancel them at the last minute when the wind speed increases and the rain risk rises. Plus, England defy my low expectations and progress beyond the group stages of June's Covid-delayed 2020 European Championship.

The next opportunity for achieving my moment of solitude doesn't come until I get an offer from George Barron to fish his home water at Nant-y-Moch. It's twelve miles north of the Teifi Pools, and if I'd bolted the opposite way along the track from Llyn Syfydrin, I'd have been there in ten minutes. At 680 acres and 1,600ft, it's the largest and highest of all the unpronounceable bodies of water I've fished so far in Wales. I look at it on Google Maps so often, its seahorse-shaped outline is burnt into my retinas, like the footage of the person in charge of our country during a global pandemic cleaning a plastic chair in a vaccination centre with a disinfectant wipe.

You could swap the chair for a world leader, a nurse suffering with PTSD or a grieving child who has lost a parent, and the result would be exactly the same. Boris Johnson may resemble a human being, or, at the very least, Gary Busey's portrayal of a shambling, incoherent, alcoholic with a toddler's haircut in *Silver Bullet*. Yet what makes a human being 'human' is entirely missing in Johnson; things like empathy, emotional intelligence, being able to vocalise your thoughts, having your photo taken without gurning and not interacting with inanimate objects or your fellow human beings like they are the Black Monolith from *2001: A Space Odessy's* Dawn of Man sequence. In fact, if I shaved Moon-Watcher, put him in a dress and tried to pass him off as my girlfriend at my school prom to avoid the ignominy of attending dateless, it still would have been a more convincing impression of a human being than anything Boris Johnson can muster.

So, whereas I briefly consider adopting the equivalent of the 'herd immunity' policy peddled by our party-loving PM at the start of the pandemic, and binge watch every werewolf film ever made in the run-up to my trip to Nant-Y-Moch, after seeing how ignoring scientific advice and continuing to shake hands with half of Twickenham worked out for him, I decide to avoid requiring the equivalent of a seven-night stay in an ICU by actually following the advice of experts.

For my Chris Whitty and JVT, read Sarah from Wales's *Fit for Adventure YouTube* channel, where she talks about 'crushing the fear demons' through a mixture of familiarisation, comfort and logic. If the fear really hits – say, if you think there's an escaped murderer outside the tent – Sarah recommends deploying her secret weapon, which is what she calls 'the logical brain.' She advises having a conversation with your inner chimp, as if you are a coach operating at a New England Patriots' Bill Belichick level of non-bullshit, and then apply their advice to de-escalate the fear gnawing at your brain like a starving rat.

The only piece of Sarah's advice that I do discard is camping out during a full moon, as it will be less dark, for obvious reasons.

It's the misty morning after the night before, and despite the champagne left unopened in the fridge, I've got a banging hangover. If nothing else, at least the lack of a mobile signal for the next two days means I'll avoid the depressing post-mortem of racism, thuggery and fuck-wittery that inevitably follows the final whistle.

The sight of George waiting for me in the car park by the dam does more for my spirits than the bacon sandwich from the Old Swan Tea Room in Rhayader. We turn the cars around, and I follow him back up the way I came, going left past a cattle grid and along a track that winds up towards the seahorse's tail. I pull up behind him in a lay-by overlooking a series of arms, points and bays formed by the Rivers Hyddgen and Rheidol entering the reservoir. A waterfall tumbles from the 2,500ft peak of Pumlumon Fawr to our right.

The track ends at a rusted gate, beyond which is an abandoned youth hostel. It looks the kind of place where the maggot-ridden corpse of the hostel's caretaker rises at night to wreak his revenge on those responsible for his death. I make a mental note of avoiding it like the fucking plague when it comes to bedding down for the night.

Not only is George, a Scotsman by birth, good enough not to mention penalties, he also shares his techniques and some more of his killer flies with me. Mirroring his set-up, I abandon my floater and string up a slow intermediate and three flies on 5lb Fulling Mill straight through. I tie a Leggy Bibio on point, Hutch's Pennell middle dropper and a Pretender on the top dropper.

The ash-coloured mud makes the top end of the reservoir feel tidal, like an estuary, and there's thirty feet between where the green hillside ends and the reservoir's edge. The wind isn't strong enough to blow any insects onto the water, so we will be the equivalent of *Deliveroo* for Nant-y-Moch's population of wild brown trout.

George turns left and follows the remains of a stone wall left behind after the hamlet of Nant-y-Moch was flooded to create the reservoir. He heads forty feet up the shore to fish down from Sheep Island, while I fish down to the mouth of the River Hyddgen. Seeing fish rising already, I cross a couple of feeder streams and head straight for the river mouth. The Hutch's Pennell is hit on the first two pulls, but what I think is a decent-sized brown trout turns out to be a double hook-up, with the second fish on the Leggy Bibio. Unlike on Chew or the Barrows, where my leader would split faster than the latest

Sugababes line-up, I manage to land and safely release both fish. The water is so clear, I can see where the silted bed of the reservoir ends and the deeper river channel begins. It's here that the fish are holding.

Following George's instructions, I lift the rod tip at the end of each pull to keep my flies continuously moving, keeping a bow in the line so the fish doesn't feel any resistance. The hook-ups continue; I've never had so many wild brownies in such a short stretch of shore. George rejoins me. He's had ten along a similar length of shore.

The Powys-Ceredigion border runs down the middle of the River Hyddgen, turns right and runs up the centre of the River Rheidol. We move from Ceredigion into Powys, and back into Ceredigion to cross the River Rheidol on zigzagging stepping stones. We catch fish after fish until the clouds roll down the side of Drogsol's south face and the biblical rain has us running for the cars.

I'm soaked through to the skin. My wellies are filled with water and it will be twenty-four hours before I experience the joys of wearing a dry pair of trousers again. I towel myself dry with a torn-up pair of boxers I use for wiping my windscreen. George gives me a dry M&S sweater that smells faintly of dogs. He shares his bar of Fruit & Nut with me.

I follow him across the dam, to where the River Ruddlan flows into the seahorses' head. Before leaving, he points out possible camping spots for tonight, and shows me where to fish tomorrow.

I decide to camp up near the abandoned youth hostel. The pitch by the hostel itself is bigger and flatter, but is a little *too* close. I settle on one overlooking Sheep Island and the bays we'd fished earlier. There's also a wire fence and gate between me and the youth hostel here, on which my trousers are currently hanging out to dry. South Korea always seems to be at the cutting edge with regard to zombie development, and four episodes into *All of Us Are Dead*, it seems the undead still aren't capable of opening doors or climbing fences, so I figure I should be safe from any vengeful reanimated caretakers. I'm also next to the waterfall, where I can wash-up, and I've gone for Sarah's 'car close by' option, rather than the 'I could leave, but my car is so far away that it's easier to stay where I am,' one. It even stops raining long enough for me to pitch the tent.

Before heading down to Sheep Island to fish the evening rise, I follow Sarah's advice and familiarise myself with anything that might look scary in the dark when I get up for a piss in the middle of the night. This includes the abandoned youth hostel, which in my head, I immediately begin writing a screenplay around for a slasher film I'm calling *The Dipping*. It's where a former caretaker, horribly disfigured from a sheep-dipping prank gone wrong, hides among the ruins of an abandoned youth hostel with a pair of over-sized shears, hell-bent on taking revenge on those he holds responsible. There's also what looks like the only bush in the entire Desert of Wales on the far side of the River Hyddgen. This convinces my inner chimp that, in an MR James-style tale of terror, it will move closer to me every time I open my tent flaps to look at it, until I know that the final time I look, the bush will be right outside my tent.

Following Sarah's advice, I give the finger to both the hostel and the malevolent bush.

On my previous attempts at overnight camping, my reading material has been deliberately beige, to avoid coming across anything that my inner chimp might seize on. No Steven King, no MR James, no Paul Tremblay, no Stephen Graham Jones, no Jack Ketchum and definitely not DLT's biography.

And yet, when I finish supper, I open up '70s nostalgia-fright fest *Scarred for Life*.

After recently rewatching *Raging Bull*, I was easily able to find online the actual footage of the eleventh round between Jake LaMotta and Sugar Ray Robinson, where LaMotta's face is reduced to *hackfleisch* as his gloves clutched the blood-splattered ropes. Likewise, when my child-actor friend Dan told me about the time he sang in an anti-child abuse video with Rolf Harris, *YouTube* was again able to come up with the jaw-droppingly ironic goods. Basically, if Kevin Costner in *Fields of Dreams* had been tasked to create a *YouTube*-style channel instead of a baseball field for dead, disgraced baseball players, the voice in the corn would have whispered: 'Upload any old shit, and someone will watch it.' Despite this, in all the years I've been online, my sporadic internet searches for footage of the *Nationwide* werewolf have failed to turn up one solitary hair.

I'd been dipping in and out of the 740-page *Scarred for Life* for months before it even occurred to me to look at the index, and there it was. The very last chapter in the book: *The Strange Case of the Nationwide Werewolf*.

What I should've been searching for all this time was the 'Hexham Heads,' which reads like a horror story much more terrifying than *The Dipping*. It starts with two young boys digging up a pair of small stone heads in their back garden in the village of Hexham. Following reports of poltergeist activity in the boys' house, and the visit of a late-night intruder, the Hexham Heads became a media sensation, being passed around various institutions to determine their origin before ending up in the hands of Dr Anne Ross, an expert in Celtic mythology. It was Dr Ross's spooky experience with the heads that formed the basis of the report on *Nationwide* that scared the living shit out of me all those years ago. During her interview, she tells of how she was woken in the night by something half-animal, half-man standing outside her bedroom door. She described it as having the body of a wolf for its upper part, while appearing human from the waist down. Then, a few days later, her daughter returned from school to be met by the werewolf jumping over a bannister and rushing towards the back of the house, before disappearing in the music room. The Hexham Heads were eventually revealed to have been made by the former occupant of the boys' house, as toys for his daughter, which brings to question not only Dr Ross's sanity, but also how a national broadcaster saw this as something to be treated seriously. As one of the legion of fellow childhood trauma victims so succinctly put it, in a thread dedicated to the *Nationwide* werewolf on the *Fortean Times* forum:

'A real fucking werewolf, on the news.'

I'm not sure how I feel about discovering that the source of my biggest childhood trauma was based upon the ravings of an unsound mind and an irresponsible broadcaster. It's not quite at the level of discovering that the 'cake was a lie' in *Portal*, or Dave Kujan connecting the dots on the noticeboard at the end of *The Usual Suspects*, but I imagine it's similar to a certain Brexit-backing, bar-owning bell-end realising after 31 January 2020 that he's got no piss-weak beer to sell to homeless people or staff to serve it.

Whatever it does, it seems to work, and I manage to sleep a whole night in the wild, solo. The waterfall helps by drowning out all sounds except for the lone honking of a Canada goose and the occasional chorus of bleating sheep. It was touch and go at one point, when I awoke around 2am in the pitch black and thoughts of what might be lurking in the abandoned youth hostel, or whether there was a sinister bush waiting for me outside my tent flaps, began to flood my mind. That was the moment I put in a mental overseas call to Bill Belichick, which went as follows:

Bill: <Indistinguishable grunt>

Ben: 'Hi Bill, I think there's a maggot-ridden corpse of a caretaker out for revenge about to rip my tent open, or maybe a malevolent bush waiting for me outside the flaps.'

Bill: 'Where are you?'

Ben: 'Nant-y-Moch.'

Bill: <Indistinguishable grunt>

Ben: 'It's like Nevada, but moorland instead of sand.'

Bill: 'When was the last time you read in the news about someone being murdered by the maggot-ridden corpse of a zombie caretaker or a malevolent bush?'

Ben: 'Does the *Daily Express* count?'

Bill: 'No.'

Ben: <long pause> ... 'Never.'

Bill: Either pack up your tent, walk past the maggot-ridden corpse of the zombie caretaker and the malevolent bush, get in your car, drive down to Ponterwyd, park under a tree and try sleeping in your passenger seat. Or, you can go to sleep.

The line goes dead.

With or without the Tom Brady GOAT factor, you can't argue with a mind that's won six Super Bowls. I rationalise that I am the only human being within ten square miles and that any other possibility is merely a product of growing up in the 70s.

I awake to sunshine, blue skies, fox gloves and solitude.

Fuck you, Frank Bough.

James B Sikking Dead

I'm watching *Capricorn One* on my MacBook Air, lying on a duvet so thick, it could have its own reality TV show on ITVBe. A conspiracy thriller about the faking of the first manned NASA mission to Mars, *Capricorn One* was the first film on my holiday playlist titled *Movies I love that I haven't seen for more than twenty-five years*. It's disappearance from the TV schedules in the mid 1990s could have been down to Jane Fonda's ex hoovering up every half-decent movie for his satellite channel, like a Chinese super-trawler. But then again, if Fred West had a supporting role in *The Darling Buds of May*, I doubt it would get many repeats on UK Gold, either.

For me, watching a film, reading a book or binge-watching a TV series has long been an interactive experience, with my mobile never far away from my TV remote or Kindle, to answer those pressing questions like, 'Where can I buy Bob Mortimer's combat jacket?'

Watching *Capricorn One* for the first time post-Google, what I want to know is if James B Sikking, who played Lieutenant Howard Hunter in *Hill Street Blues*, and currently has his finger poised over a big red button, is still alive. Trouble is, there's no Wi-Fi or mobile signal in the crofter's cottage, and the only telly I'll watch all week is the one flying a red crop duster while yelling "Perverts!" at crashing helicopters. I'll also spend the first two days at 252 Culkein slicing tomatoes with a kitchen knife the length of a machete on a dinner plate, because I can't find where the smaller blades or chopping board are kept. I still haven't found the pig bin for food scraps, which is troubling me, since I'm now down to the crusts on the loaf of white sliced bread I bought in Ullapool on Saturday, and I know I will go to climate change hell if I throw them in the black bin. Ditto the clothes pegs, and the immersion heater only produces enough hot water to warm the back of my thighs when having a bath. There's also the matter of my towel refusing to stay on the towel rail, a red folder that falls from the middle of the table in the hall, and a dining chair that moves 45° away from the table each night, which all has me seriously considering calling in the local exorcist. On the plus side, the crofter's cottage is warm. It's got one of those bathroom stools with the cork lid, a can opener that's fixed to the wall, and there's a tiny mouse that lives between the bristles on the bottom of the front door.

The lack of a mobile signal and Wi-Fi at 252 Culkein means that each day's fishing starts with me parking outside the 1909 house. It's at a crossroads on a hill above Culkein and it's the only place in the area I can get a mobile signal on the UK's shittiest network. Turning right at the crossroads will take you to Stoer Head Light House and beyond that, the Old Man of Stoer, rising from the ocean like the 200ft high middle finger I'd like to give every motorhome clogging up the NC500. Built from the local sandstone, the 1909 house is a picture of symmetry. There are identical chimneys at either end of the slate roof, three narrow rectangular windows built into the eaves, and two more windows either side of the porch on the ground floor. It seems less abandoned and more like a time capsule; its interior hermetically sealed around about the time I last watched *Capricorn One* on TV. The pitted sandstone walls, faded red paint on the front door, rusted drainpipes and peeling window frames make me wonder how much longer it can withstand the elements. This close to the Atlantic, every empty building is only one broken window and a hooley away from becoming the local Marsten House.

As well as discovering if James B Sikking is still alive and ticking, I need a mobile signal to access the interactive Google map and itineraries that Stewart Yates, the local fishing guide, has created for me. Like Planet Earth, three quarters of Assynt's surface is water, and even a cursory glance at OS Explorer Map 442 reveals the impossibility of me trying to determine the Tony Hancocks from the Matt Hancocks with only seven days available to fish. Stewart's map is a marvel of minimalist design. There are just ten red icons with a white fish's head that are the 'X' marks the spot on my Assynt treasure map. Touching an individual icon brings up a brief description, such as 'Stunning location,' 'Big fish,' 'Lots of fish' and 'Worth the slog.' I also have to factor in the weather, distance, parking, how far I'll have to walk, how many motorhomes I'll have to give way to and how many more breakfasts I'll get out of my supply of Lorne Sausage before I have to go to Lochinver.

Stewart's map is the Mrs Spencer to my Alberto the Frog, only with each day offering a dizzying array of fishing possibilities, rather than flavours of milkshakes. Be it in a boat, bank, stream or spot for stalking spooky beasts, it's eerie how accurate the green lines are on Stewart's map. Caught in the crosshairs of GPS satellites orbiting the Earth, I find myself walking along them in real time as I track my progress on the screen of my Nokia, the blue dot becoming my virtual equivalent of 'Are we there yet?'

Any map, no matter how good, is only ever a means of getting you to your destination, and I soon realise that when it comes to the actual fishing, it's like wearing a face mask north of Charnock Richard services. I am on my own.

There are, of course, the true artists among those who fish for wild brownies in remote upland llyns and lochs, like Stewart himself, and Wales' George Barron. However, when fishing for the equivalent of a fat lad awaiting his first *Deliveroo* after a national lockdown, I find an artisan approach of a handful of confidence flies and covering a lot of water will usually be enough to get me some fish.

The electronic signs on the A74 on the way up to Assynt read: 'Fasten Seatbelts,' which I assumed made reference to the quality of the fishing that lay ahead. But after driving seven hundred miles, dumping the contents of my car in a heap on the floor of 252 Culkein and blanking on Loch Cul Fraoich, I'm beginning to worry that the messages did, in fact, refer to Scottish driving habits. Two hours into fishing Loch Poll the next day, and persisting with something leggy on point, a Pennell on the middle dropper and something bushy on the bob, I still haven't caught my first Assynt brownie. It's only when the cloud ceiling drops, the rain hammers down and I lose sight of Quinag's three peaks that I'm forced into making a change. No sooner have I put a Wickhams Fancy on the point to anchor my cast and fish a little deeper than my line tightens. I find myself holding my first fish of the holiday, with the same sense of delirious anticipation as every time I hear Brian Moore yelling, "It's up for grabs now!"

One evening, I return to 252 Culkein to discover that I've become a one-man County Lines gang. Accidentally leaving the gate at the bottom of the drive open in the morning, the garden is now filled with the local sheep grazing on the lushest, freshest and greenest grass this side of Ullapool. Having had their free sample, I shoo them out. When they come back tomorrow, I'll charge them £20 a head; thirty for the cattle who come down off the hills into the village on Thursday nights. A couple of days later, something takes a dump on the path between the front door and the boot of my car, which I tread in and then track down the hallway carpet. I put this down to the black sheep with R3 sprayed on its side, rather than poltergeist activity. R3 has attitude. Unlike the others, she doesn't run away when I appear in the window first thing in the morning. Instead, she freezes, as if staying still will render her invisible to all humans, all the while watching me from the corner of her eye.

Aware that every second I spend gazing at my phone is a second's less time spent fishing, I limit my morning internet sessions outside the 1909 house to only what's essential to the day's fishing. Needing to know the temperature, wind speed, wind direction and air pressure for my journal, I'm Googling 'Yesterday's weather forecast.' Of course, I already know what the weather was like yesterday, because I fished in it. It was the exactly the kind of weather in which you shouldn't take a solo boat out on a large loch that lies on a westerly bearing, a couple of miles inland from the Atlantic. Unfortunately, because I forgot to check the weather forecast yesterday morning, that's exactly what I did.

Beannach is the first of the three itineraries that Stewart prepared for me, and it was always going to be my boat day. The itineraries offer more detail than the Google map, including parking, detailed routes of the walk in and, most importantly, hotspots of where the best fishing is. On Beannach, this is mostly between the atoll of wooded islands at the eastern end of the loch, but just as there are some kids who should be kept away from sharp objects, there are also fishermen that should be kept away from solo rowboats.

Rowing down to the islands, the combination of the boat's low seat and huge oars already has me feeling like Ruprecht sitting at eye-level with the dining table, while eating his applesauce with a corked fork. My set-up is the same as on Loch Poll, and as the day warms, the brownies that inhabit the water between the islands move up my cast from the Wickhams until they start coming exclusively to the Yellow Tail Bibio on the top dropper. At that point, I switch the Wickhams for a Bibio Hopper with an orange tail, which accounts for its own fair share of a catch rate that is accelerating like a T20 run chase. I even have a double hook-up with what look like identical twins, both over 12", and I manage to bring them both to the boat despite having forgotten my landing net.

With Suilven to my back and Quinag in front, I drift along the far fern-covered bank into a bay. The pond weed as the bay shallows remind me of Home Loch on Jura, where I caught my biggest fish of that holiday, and history repeats itself as I shake free from the dropper a fish that has woofed the Yellow Tail Bibio, and stretches from my fingertips to halfway up my forearm.

After lunch I attempt to row up to the top end of the loch where a throbbing red hotspot on Stewart's itinerary beckons. I know I'm in trouble when the next time I look over my right shoulder, Suilven has disappeared. Then, the wind picks up. Feeling the pressure dropping and my forward motion becoming non-existent, I moor the boat, take off my life jacket, walk half a mile up the shore and fish my way back down. With takes drying up, I switch the Bibio back with the Wickhams and again find fish. The wind is gusting now and all I want to do is get the boat and myself back safely to the relatively sheltered inlet where the moorings are. It's only when I try to retrieve the leader caught under the boat that I realise I forgot to put my lifejacket back on. I then compound the situation by knocking one of the oars from the rowlocks. All the interactive maps in the world can't replace the services of a decent ghillie, or at the very least an outboard motor, and such is my shame that I wait until I have the cover of darkness before posting the boat key through the letterbox of the DIY shop in Lochinver.

Apart from losing access to Stewart's map and the lack of forward planning, I don't miss the lack of Wi-Fi and mobile signal in 252 Culkein. At home, my day starts and ends in front of a laptop screen. Here, my day is bookended with me sitting in an electric-blue wing-back chair, my feet resting on a tartan footstool, drinking a coffee (morning) or root beer (evening) while looking out the window at David's house and Culkein Bay beyond. David's house is on the other side of a stream that separates him from the road on its way to emptying into the bay. He rescues unwanted sheep dogs that have been mistreated or can no longer be looked after by their owners. His current brood is four: a young pup who he's going to train to be a working dog, an old mum who was chained up and used solely for breeding, an Australian shepherd who is barking to be let out of its wire enclosure, and a collie with a white head and black body who's obsessed with quad bikes.

David is not to be confused with Dave, a designer from Shropshire, who has been coming to Culkein since he was eight. Dave fishes from the bay in a kayak, and drops off freshly caught mackerel for David's BBQ. With a cigarette permanently attached to the corner of his mouth, milky-blue eyes, tight curls and legs that couldn't trap a pig in an alleyway, Dave's the spit of Moxy from *Auf Weidersehen Pet*. On my first evening, David reels off a list of places to fish that I'm too embarrassed to ask him to repeat, and I know that if I ever lose my mobile signal all together, I'll never be able to find them on my OS map with my own phonetic spelling. I never do find out what he does for a living, but the back of his battered white Ford Transit flatbed suggests that he's Culkein's man with a van, performing every role from removals to roofing, to local knacker man.

I only make the mistake of deviating from Stewart's green lines once. It's my second itinerary day and I'm supposed to be fishing my way up a 'wee burn' to a small loch. I set up a 7'6" 3WT, with a single tungsten head nymph on the point. My 5wt is strapped to my backpack, to be broken out once I reach the small loch. After picking up a handful of tiny brownies in the first pool, the stretch of water ahead looks too skinny to hold any fish, so I step out of the stream and begin making my way along the bank. The ground begins to rise sharply, I can't see any obvious deer trails to follow, and what starts off as gentle stroll quickly turns into an SAS route march. The sun is out for the first time on the holiday, and stripped down to a red T-shirt, I'll be bearing the scars of the insect bites, tics and scratches from gorse and bracken as a reminder of this day long after the tan has faded from my arms.

After reaching what I thought to be the highest rise, I look up and see hundreds more feet to climb in front of me, and the face of a seemingly impassable waterfall. While the terrain's not as steep as the cliff face that Sam Waterston climbs in *Capricorn One* while telling the one about the dead cat, and it's not as hot as the dried-up riverbed that the stabby former running back of the Buffalo Bills digs for water in, if there happened to be a couple of olive-coloured helicopters circling overhead, I'd gladly hold my hands up and let them take me to wherever it is all the 'disappeared' end up. I'm at breaking point. I can't go on another step, and am seriously considering turning around and heading back to the car.

The stream now lies at the bottom of a gorge 150ft

below me. There's a tumble of giant blocks of granite forming the kind of deep, black fishy pools you'd only expect to see in New Zealand. My inner chimp reminds me that New Zealand is eleven and a half thousand miles and twenty-four hours on a plane away, which makes it as likely a destination for me as the surface of Mars. I offer a silent prayer before sliding down the sheer grassy side of the ravine on my arse, and splash land in the stream below like an Apollo capsule.

Walking back out along the top of the ravine in the evening, I'll realise that I was only one rocky outcrop away from the trail flattening out and a reasonably easy walk to the small loch. My reward for showing a level of fortitude and never-say-die attitude that would have made a rattlesnake-munching James Brolin proud, is the sheer joy of rock-hopping my way up the ravine, getting to bathe beneath a set of triple falls and, on the small loch, witnessing my first rise of the holiday before taking a dozen trout in a mad sixty minutes, all of which are more than 14". Then, it's over as quickly as it started, and the clouds and low-pressure system that roll in will stay until the end of the holiday. Still, the rain is kind enough to hold off until I'm queuing for fish and chips from the mobile chippy parked by the sand dunes in Clachtoll.

Having climbed to a combined height of 1,800ft and walked close to 20km, I forego my seat in the wing back armchair and drink my bottle of root beer in the bath. Wanting to give my aching muscles a proper soak, I leave the immersion heater on when I get into the bath, and hope that the water tank will reheat quickly enough for me to cover my nipples with hot water before hyperthermia sets in.

That evening, the wind changes direction and blows onto the back of the cottage. There's a familiar *ping* as my phone shows the first sign of life so far between the walls of 252 Culkein. I Google to see if sheep can eat bread, if I can eat Lochinver Larder's Pies cold, and what a Greenland shark looks like. I then switch it off, as I already have everything I need for tomorrow's fishing.

On my way down to the bay, I feed the two crusts of bread to R3. She doesn't know it yet, but I'm charging £5 per slice of the loaf I'm going to buy in the local Spar tomorrow.

In the gloom, I see David's flatbed on the beach, backed up with the tailgate against the side of the concrete slipway. The tip of Dave's cigarette glows in the darkness. He's wedging a wooden beam in the gap between the tailgate and the top of the slipway, making a ramp. David is behind the wheel of an an ancient red tractor parked on the slipway. In pitch darkness, guided only by the glow of Dave's cigarette, he reverses the tractor off the slipway and onto the back of his flatbed.

In the morning, he'll deliver the tractor to Lochinver for its annual service.

James B Sikking is eighty-seven years old.

CASTLE E-MOVIE STORYBOARDS

Castle Intro Storyboard

Project: Crossfire	PIVOTAL GAMES	Timeline:	Time Of day:
Scene: Castle - Intro E-movie		Weather:	Sky:
Total Duration:		Lighting:	

Shot No: 1	Duration:	Camera: 1	Shot No: 2	Duration:	Camera: 1	Shot No: 3	Duration:	Camera: 2

Action: Screen fades up from Black.

Establishing shot of the Castle entrance and far vista.

The location and time teletypes into the bottom left of the screen.

Sound Effects:
Howling wind.
Text:
Location and Time Text: "Kolyma Castle, Siberia. 02:34am"

Action: The camera slowly tilts down to reveal the drawbridge. Two New Cheka guards patrol up and down the drawbridge.

Sound Effects:
Howling Wind. Rustling trees.
Dialogue:

Action: The camera cuts close up of a grappling hook and climbing rope. Hook is embedded on the edge of a forested plateau that overlooks the vista. A full moon shines down.

Sound Effects:
Howling Wind. Rustling trees.
Dialogue:
Laing (off) "You know your eye-brows meet in the middle, Bro'?"

Project: Crossfire	PIVOTAL GAMES	Timeline:	Time Of day: Night-time
Scene: Castle - Intro E-movie		Weather: Windy, cold.	Sky:
Total Duration:		Lighting: Dark	

Shot No: 4	Duration:	Camera: 2	Shot No: 5	Duration:	Camera: 3	Shot No: 6	Duration:	Camera: 3

Action: The camera quickly pulls out to show Laing equipping his light machine gun and Walsh crouched in a kneeling position on top of the plateau. Walsh then moves up and out of frame right, Laing begins to follow.

Sound Effects:
Howling Wind. Rustling trees. Drunken soldiers shouting.

Dialogue:
Laing (cont) "Full moon tonight."

Action: Cut to close up of empty vodka bottles lined up on a rock. Each of the bottles are shot away one by one, from left to right revealing the New Cheka soldiers camped around the fire behind.

Sound Effects:
Howling Wind. Rustling trees.

Action: Two of the soldiers are sat down drunk. One is singing badly, the other egging him on. The third is still shooting at the last bottle.

Sound Effects:
Howling Wind. Rustling trees.

Project: Crossfire	PIVOTAL GAMES	Timeline:	Time Of day: Night-time
Scene: Castle - Intro E-movie		Weather: Windy, cold	Sky:
Total Duration:		Lighting: Dark	

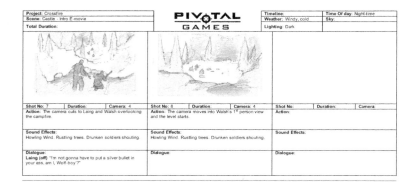

Shot No: 7	Duration:	Camera: 4	Shot No: 8	Duration:	Camera: 4	Shot No:	Duration:	Camera:

Action: The camera cuts to Laing and Walsh overlooking the campfire.

Sound Effects:
Howling Wind. Rustling trees. Drunken soldiers shouting.

Dialogue:
Laing (off) "I'm not gonna have to put a silver bullet in your ass, am I, Wolf-boy'?"

Action: The camera moves into Walsh's 1st person view and the level starts.

Sound Effects:
Howling Wind. Rustling trees. Drunken soldiers shouting.

Dialogue:

Action:

Sound Effects:

Dialogue:

Cheese

I was the writer on one of the worst video games ever made. *Conflict: Denied Ops* was a bad game even before *Call of Duty 4* came out five months before its release date, sold zillions of copies and rewrote the rules for first-person shooters (FPS). *Denied Ops'* improbable globe-trotting plot involved a South American dictator and a stolen nuke, back in those innocent pre-pandemic, pre-climate change, pre-Trump days when a stolen nuke in the hands of a South American dictator was the scariest shit that could happen. It was an FPS with a co-op twist, where you controlled two CIA operatives: Graves, a sniper; and heavy weapons specialist Laing. You could play as either character, while simultaneously ordering the non-playing one to advance or provide covering fire, with the option to hot-swap between the two at any time. There was also the option of teaming up with a friend and playing it as a split screen co-op campaign.

This was how the head of the studio and the producer chose to play it. They spent hours sitting up in their office with headsets on, talking to each other as they cleared a level as if they were SEAL Team Six storming Bin Laden's compound. Trouble is, when it was released, no one else played it that way, if they even played it at all. As a result, they were the only two out of one hundred and twenty-three employees who were surprised by the universally awful reviews when it was released.

I'm currently wishing I was part of a two-man squad, with my wingman positioned up high among the tussocks on one of the hills overlooking the loch I'm fishing. Even with my Oakley's on, at shore level, I can't see anything through the mercury-like surface of the water. We could wear headsets like the studio head and the senior producer, and say things like, 'Brownie one bravo at your six.' Them being armed with a sniper's rifle complete with a scope powerful enough to individually take out the midges swarming around my head would be even better, although having penetrated a gallon of Avon skin-so-soft and my face net, it wouldn't surprise me if the bitey little feckers turned out to be bullet-proof as well.

The loch is in Assynt, and out of respect to local fishing guide Stewart Yates, I'm going to be as vague about its location as Nicky Minaj was about exactly whose testicles swelled up after receiving their Covid vaccination. According to the description on Stewart's interactive Google map, it's a 'big fish loch,' and by big fish, he means wild brownies up to 5lbs. He also tells me over the phone that it should be fished with 'extreme stealth.'

'Imagine you're trying to creep up on an SAS sniper who knows you're coming, and will blow your head off if they detect you.'

It's not just because of the potential FOAL that I'm fishing BFL today. On the map, it's also the shortest walk-in of all the locations that I've yet to fish, and according to what I can see on my Nokia, it looks the least likely to give me a coronary. I've fished every day since leaving home seven days ago, including a session on Blencarn Lake outside Penrith on the drive up; climbed a combined elevation equal to scaling Suilven; and rolled more miles than the Proclaimers over ground so rough it makes Sean Dyche sound like the Cadbury's Caramel Bunny. I'm now beginning to suspect that I may have hit the fishing equivalent of 'the wall' that usually occurs nine or ten days into a lads' or ladettes' holiday in Magaluf, when your genitals resemble a Dulux paint chart, your liver looks like Gordon Ramsey's face and the thought of another night of San Franciscos with John Travolta and Mama Maria before hitting Tokyo Joe's sees you turning your hotel bedsheet into the Turin Shroud.

True to Stewart's map, the walk is, by Assynt standards, short. It's also steep, and for most of the climb, my face is pressed into the heather covering the near vertical slope. Luckily, I'm travelling light, swapping backpack for sling pack and waders for waterproof trousers and wellies. I say luckily, as that is probably all that prevents me from being airlifted out on a gurney by the mountain rescue service. If there was a *Rocky V-style* training montage marking the narrative arc of my preparation for the holiday, culminating in me heroically scrambling up the ridge in front of me, it would consist of two shots: me lying on my sofa scratching myself while eating from a bag of Chocolate Buttons balanced on my chest, and me on my hands and knees on top of the cliff over-looking BFL and dry-heaving.

My reaction to looking out across BFL and seeing the flat calm is the same as Indiana Jones's when seeing that the floor of the Well of Souls is a living carpet of deadly snakes:

'Why did it have to be a flat calm?'

The lack of a wind isn't only bad news because of the microscopic ninjas devouring me, or because it makes the chance of spooking already spooky fish even likelier, but also because Stewart was very specific about the tactics for fishing BFL. Namely, cast a dry fly six to ten feet out from the bank and leave it there.

Even more terrifying than the midges, and my diminishing chances of making my way around BFL undetected without Andy McNab headshotting me with an M107, is the thought of having to leave a fly still on the water. The only time I fish a dry fly these days is when the street lights are on along the A38, and the Barrows are fizzing with rising trout like someone's dumped a giant Alka-Seltzer in the water.

Since arriving in Assynt, I've been exclusively fishing Scottish Loch-style, with a slow-sinking line and a cast of three wet flies. Even on Blencarn, I only started catching when I realised the rainbows wanted a damsel nymph stripped through the surface. The motion of strip, lift-rod-tip, strip, lift-rod-tip, hang flies, cast, has become so ingrained that I don't know what to do with my hands, so I alternate between sticking them under my armpits or sitting on them. I briefly consider taking off my face net and letting the midges crawl all over me, just so I'll have something else to keep my hands busy. All the while, my leader and elk hair caddis shrivel on the surface, like a time-lapse of a decomposing vampire, before drifting limply into the shore. For me, it's too much like float-fishing. Plus, I feel a complete tit Indian-crawling my way around the loch to the sound of my inner Nelson Muntz pointing at me and going, 'Ha-ha!'

I give it twenty more minutes and then drive into Lochinver to stock up on Lorne sausage.

In terms of the challenge Stewart set me, fishing BFL felt more like a video game designed by Hidetaka Miyazaki than one designed on a former chicken farm outside Bath. The difference being that *Denied Ops'* sniper and heavy machine gun combo could be played however you wanted, whereas be it *Dark Souls*, *Bloodborne* or *Sekiro*, if it's a Hidetaka Miyazaki game you play, it's his way or the highway. Try to rush a group of Huntsmen instead of taking them on one at a time? Dead. And don't even think about trying to take on a Black Knight until you've mastered the riposte or backstab.

The only way to progress through a Hidetaka Miyazaki game is by killing bosses. Every time you die fighting a boss, you learn a little bit more about that boss's move set and the best strategy to counter them. Take on a boss enough times, and you eventually develop a rhythm where you are able to dodge their attacks, begin to get your counters in and whittle down their health enough to eventually take them down. Ask me what the greatest moment of my life was within ear shot of my partner and I'll tell you it was the birth of our daughter. Out of ear shot, it's Mickey Thomas in the last minute at Anfield in 1989. However, put a gun to my head, and I'll confess that the feeling of finally beating *Dark Soul's* Ornstein and Smough at what felt like the five hundred and eighteenth attempt, runs both of the aforementioned far too close for any middle-aged man to ever admit.

The yin to the euphoric yang of finally defeating a particularly impossible boss is hitting the glass ceiling in terms of your ability or skillset and being unable to kill them. The soul-destroying, hair-tearing, rage-quitting reality of repeatedly taking on a boss and dying hundreds of times is like every time you've been broken off by a big fish because your fly line got wrapped around your reel handle to the power of infinity, ad infinitum. This is where the cheese comes in.

In gaming circles, 'cheese' or 'cheesing' is used to describe a way of defeating a boss that isn't dependent on skill, but is instead done through exploiting a glitch in the level design or the boss's mechanics. In my defence, I will say that, driven by my pathological obsession to defeat every boss in every game I play, I've only ever cheesed optional bosses. These are bosses that you don't have to defeat to progress through the game, and who, by their very nature, are always the hardest to beat.

Take *Sekiro's* Demon of Hatred for example. The Demon of Hatred is a horned, pissed off, 100ft-high orangutang with a flaming left arm. The traditional strategy to defeat him requires staying underneath him and dodging his foot stomps, jump attacks, headbutts and charges, and basically whacking his nads with a samurai sword. He's also a three-phase boss, meaning you have to deplete his health bar three times, and each time the demon dies it grows more powerful. In phase two, he will start smashing his flaming arm to the ground, causing the area in front of him to catch fire, in addition to flinging fire balls. Phase three will see the fire balls become homing fire balls and he will also start spinning to create a whirling circle of fire that instantly incinerates you.

The trick is to learn the tells that signal which attack is about to be launched, and then make the correct counter move. The trouble is that if you jump when you should've dodged left, dodge left when you should've jumped, are off with your timing by a millisecond, miss a grapple attack or get too greedy with hitting the demon in his swingers, it's instant death.

The thing that always strikes me when watching a cheese video is how people come up with the cheese in the first place. I mean, what is the thought process that leads to someone discovering how you can lure the Demon of Hatred behind the bough of a barren Sakura Tree, where it becomes stuck, and then that the body of a dead horse on the other side of the tree marks the limit of the Demon's ranged attacks, from which you can run forward, jab him with your sword once and safely retreat back behind the dead horse, rinsing and repeating to whittle away his health bar until he dies? Like Chris Yates waking up one morning and deciding to dress as a scarecrow to catch Redmire's carp, these cheese merchants are true trailblazers, clearly operating at another level to mere mortals like me.

It took me twenty-three minutes and numerous attempts, but after finally killing the giant, hairy orange bastard, I celebrated as if an all-in-one device had been invented that eradicates Covid, reverses the effects of climate change, clears our rivers of shit, closes the chicken farms along the River Wye, ends open-cage salmon farming and keeps Jose Mourinho permanently unemployed.

It's the lack of silence, more than the noise, that wakes me in the darkness. Apart from the occasional sheep rubbing itself against the white pebble-dashed walls of 252 Culkein in the night, there's a complete absence of the ambient noises that provides my usual night-time non-soundtrack. I've grown so used to the silence that at first, I can't even identify the noise coming from the back of the cottage. Then, I realise it's rain, accompanied by a howling wind strong enough to rattle the single-pane windows in their frames.

It's Saturday morning, my car is packed and it's kicking out time at the crofter's cottage. The storm lashing the back of 252 Culkein with the torrential rain that woke me up at 5am still rages and has put paid to fishing any of the unfished lochs on Stewart's map on the way to my AIRBnB in Inverness.

Except one.

In some ways, the spooky giant brownies of BFL are the ultimate optional boss. I mean, I don't have to catch one; I can just get in my car, drive to Inverness and spend a relaxing afternoon, warm and dry, browsing in Leakey's bookshop, followed by dirty fries and a BBQ Beef in Coyote Burger. However, just as I'm obsessed with defeating every boss in every game I play, I'm never going to pass up the opportunity of catching a FOAL, and the change in the weather has provided me with the perfect opportunity to cheese BFL.

The deer trail I climbed two days ago is now a gushing mountain stream. I'm travelling even lighter than last time, with just a net, a bottle of water, a spool of 8lb leader, snippers and a single fly box. My 7wt is strung up with a clear intermediate and a grizzle snake fly. I hope that the combination of driving rain and gale force wind will also provide enough cover for me to get away with the bright-yellow raincoat I'm wearing.

On the opposite side of the slope, I'm sheltered from the worst of the wind gusting against the cliff face, but the roaring grows louder with each step nearer to the top. The wind is being funnelled down the loch from the north, causing white-capped waves to break against the foot of the cliff; the spray and foam transforming the tumps surrounding the loch into a pod of killer whales chasing seals onto a beach. In the washed-out landscape of green, grey and purple, the berries on the rowan tree in the bottom right-hand corner of the loch stand out like a homicidal dwarf in a red raincoat among the canals of Venice.

Denied Ops was doomed from the minute the American corporation that owned the studio decided to change it from the third-person shooter format, which had been so successful in previous Conflict games, to cash in on the FPS craze. In doing so, they alienated the Conflict franchise's fan base, and *Denied Ops* was left to shuffle almost unnoticed under a bar that had been raised so high by *Call of Duty 4*.

For my own sins, I struggled with the transition from writing for the big screen to writing for the console. Where previously I'd been the creator of the blueprint for the house, I was now the painter-and-decorator tasked with covering up a giant cock and balls chiselled into the walls of the master bedroom, just as the new owners pulled up on the drive outside.

In aiming for a classic '80s buddy movie aesthetic, where the grizzled vet and cocky rookie's antipathy for each other mellows over time into a mutual respect, I'd failed to take into account the fact that whereas your average Hollywood movie has at least ninety minutes to establish the characters and play out their respective arcs, in *Denied Ops*, I had roughly three and half minutes of cutscenes. The resulting characterisation was less an arc than a tedious, ten-hour-long straight line, consisting of a large black man and an older white man continuously yelling abuse at each other, with a high-five at the end as they pack General Ramirez off to Guantanamo Bay in an orange jumpsuit.

Lethal Weapon it was not.

My penance was to pour over every lousy review of the game and every forum post in the vain hope of a positive mention of either the dialogue or characterisation. Luckily, writers are thought even less of in the video games industry than they are in the film business, so I emerged pretty much unscathed; unlike the studio, which was shut down three months later.

Yet, even movies as bad as *Showgirls* can attract a cult following, and now, thirteen years after its release, there are still new walkthroughs for *Denied Ops* going up online, with people sharing fond memories of playing the game during their childhoods. I'm pretty sure that somewhere, there's also a dark corner of the internet dedicated to weirdos who like to fish dries in flat calms for giant, spooky brownies in midge-infested waters.

Me? I'll be the George Denbrough lookalike with the 7wt and grizzle snake, standing astride a 100ft cliff in Assynt, in a hooley, feeling like a sexual tyrannosaurus.

'For God and country – Geronimo, Geronimo, Geronimo.'

Epilogue

Now we're at the end, in the spirit of *Fuller House*, the question is, did we learn something, and do we love each other?

Me? I'm no longer afraid of the dark and I learnt that whatever might lurk there is just a product of my over-active imagination, unless it's Dave Lee-Travis.

I'm writing this in a wooden goods wagon, in a Welsh valley so remote, it could have Doug McClure battling dinosaurs in it. There's no electricity or running water, and I'm living out every *Desolation Angel* fantasy I've ever had.

Although I did pass an overgrown farmhouse with dumped cars outside that could belong to missing hitchhikers.

I'm also getting Spahn Movie Ranch vibes from the commune I'm staying in, which I suspect might be run by a Manson-worshipping hippy death cult.

Plus, I'm two cans into my three-can limit of Evil Juice, and it's a long walk down the hill across the fields to the toilets.

There's a full moon.

And it's very, very dark outside.

About the Author

Ben Jailler is a regular contributor to *Fly Culture* and *Fallon's Angler*, and has also written for *Flyfish Journal* and *Trout & Salmon*. He graduated from Bournemouth University with a BA in Screenwriting for Film and Television, and has written screenplays, video games and worked in media production. Ben lives in the South West of England and counts the days between his road trips to fish for wild brown trout in remote Lochs and Llyns.

Fishhooksfurcoats.wordpress.com
Twitter: @FHandFC
Facebook: Ben Jailler
Instagram: fhandfc

Printed in Great Britain
by Amazon

14946831R00079